The Lady Is Delicate

The Lady Is Delicate
An Italian Villa Memoir

Sallie Sinclair Maclay

Illustrated by the Author

Edited by Elisabeth Hallett

iUniverse
New York and Bloomington

The Lady Is Delicate
An Italian Villa Memoir

iUniverse books may be ordered through booksellers or by contacting:

iUniverse
1663 Liberty Drive
Bloomington, IN 47403
www.iuniverse.com
1-800-Authors (1-800-288-4677)

ISBN: 978-1-4502-2892-3 (sc)
ISBN: 978-1-4502-2893-0 (ebook)

Printed in the United States of America

iUniverse rev. date: 4/26/2010

Acknowledgment

Thank you to Nick Hallett for many, many hours of technical help that made it possible for us to include Sallie's own charming illustrations.

Foreword

This memoir is so ahead of its time—written fifty years before the current deluge of books on everybody's experience in Italy.

The period is the time shortly after the end of World War II, known in Italy as the *dopoguerra*. A few military souvenirs turn up—the gas mask, the pistol—but mostly the focus is on domestic situations and events seen in a humorous light (at least at a distance!).

Family members and a few friends have enjoyed these reminiscences from time to time in manuscript, so we have finally decided to give them a more permanent and accessible form, as a memorial to Sallie, our Mother.

~ Marta and Elisabeth

TABLE OF CONTENTS

1

God Moves the Furniture

The thing is probably hereditary in the female genes, an incurable and universal affliction of womankind that manifests itself by periodic and often violent moving about of the family furniture. Certainly it recurs at regular intervals in most households—with a fever of activity and a rash of inconveniences, as any husband will testify—and in our own, it once threatened the very foundation of our domestic bliss.

I come of a long line of furniture shifters, probably dating back to the time the first cave woman shoved the first stone a little bit nearer the fire and slung the bearskin in *that* corner of the cave.

My husband, on the other hand, is descended from a torpid Calabrian strain of God-fearing ancestors who, if a fig tree sprouted in the center of the dirt floor, patiently beat a path around it. Frank has an innate conviction that however the furniture was first placed in a room is the way it permanently belongs, even if it's just the way the movers happened to leave it. This, naturally, over the course of some fifteen years of sharing the same house—and always a house where someone else has had first whack at the arrangement—has led to some pretty bitter scenes.

When I was young and optimistic (and this brings me right down almost to the present), I used to think that if I moved things while Frank was away he would come home and be pleasantly surprised at the improvement I had wrought, and would accept the *fait accompli* with good grace if not with enthusiasm. I was always wrong, for whenever he returned to our threshold and discerned even the slightest deviation in the location of movable objects, his face took on the expression of an early Christian martyr and he either sulked for days or dramatized his annoyance by barking his shins on a displaced chair.

Neither of these procedures ever alleviated in the slightest my congenital weakness for rearrangement, and my persistence eventually paid off in an unexpected and gratifying manner. History has been on my side, and certain events have not only served to soften my husband's attitude but have caused him to regard my instinct for the placement of furniture as well-nigh supernatural.

The last time I shifted the furniture—surreptitiously, that is— was that time shortly after the war, in Italy, when the jeep was almost stolen, and even Frank now admits that my changing of the domestic landscape was highly fortuitous, though at the time he would only swear eloquently under his breath and mutter, "You *would* move things around when my back was turned!"

It was the day Frank was due back to Rome, from a six-week assignment covering the U.S. task force on maneuvers in the Mediterranean, that I finally gathered energy to do what I had contemplated doing for a long time, namely to remove from our bedroom a delicate and, from my point of view, totally useless period-piece of a lady's writing desk. What I wanted in the bedroom instead was something less beautiful but more functional, a bureau with large, capacious drawers in which to stow away our belongings.

Italian houses are notably lacking in both closets and bureaus. They have, instead, a formidable species of closet-on-legs known as an *armadio*, or wardrobe, which is generally so high that coat hangers are made with long stems to hoist the garments up. They have, also, numerous little wormy inlaid pieces whose drawers are barely big enough to accommodate handkerchiefs, and they have massive carved caskets whose hinged tops are raised and lowered at the risk of hernia, sprained ligaments, and broken bones. But a good big smooth-sliding, four-drawer chest is practically nonexistent.

In the country villa which we were occupying, however, there was, in one of the unused rooms, a fine big bureau on the top of which stood two great bell-jars covering sprays of artificial flowers in ornately gilded vases, an antique horror which had caused me to retreat hastily from this room when it was revealed to me on my first conducted tour of the house. We had lived in the villa for six months or so before I gathered courage to tell the man, Bandini, to pack these atrocities off to the attic, thus liberating the bureau for my utilitarian ends.

The twinge I felt as I watched Bandini teetering up the dark attic stairs with these relics was not of conscience for having disturbed a generations-long arrangement, but arose from the harrowing knowledge that they were listed on our inventory at 35,000 lire each— at a moment when the lira stood 250 to the dollar.

The transfer of the bell-jars I had accomplished some time back, on the pretext that the fragile confections beneath them (while undoubtedly priceless and very beautiful if you like that sort of thing) might be a temptation to the children—our six-year-old and his own eight-year-old—a pair of light-hearted brigands whose taste for exploring the intricacies of the big house was well known to both of us.

The actual moving of the furniture was a different matter. For this kind of undertaking, bound to have certain repercussions, the opportunity had to ripen. Frank's assignment on the Mediterranean cruise was obviously heaven-sent, though destiny's wires were slightly crossed in the matter of afflicting me simultaneously with all the agues of early pregnancy. It was not until the final hours before his return that I felt up to my project.

On the morning in question I summoned my minions and outlined the plan of campaign. The big commode in the *camera da ospiti*, as the room was euphemistically called (though one would never have considered putting any guest in such an antique chamber of horrors), was to be brought into our bedroom. The desk was to be put in the *anticamera* of the guest room. There were other details such as removing festoons of cobwebs from the wall and the back of the bureau, and fetching something up from the storeroom to compensate the guest room for its all too obvious loss, but these were the essentials, and with no more than the usual amount of advice and imprecations among the help, the job was accomplished.

It was with a sense of considerable triumph that I collected our belongings from various shelves and chests here and there about the house and arranged them systematically in the big bureau, all dusted and be-papered inside. In an appeasing spirit, I gave over the two top drawers to my husband's things while I took for myself the less desirable lower ones, a wifely touch which I doubt he ever appreciated in view of what happened that night.

In the late afternoon came the awaited phone call from the office in Rome, word that my voyager had survived the rigors of six splendid weeks on the Mediterranean. He would be home to our slightly rakish nest on Monte Mario, the highlands overlooking Rome, in time for dinner, which means anywhere from eight o'clock on.

Upon his arrival there was the usual accumulated flood of talk to be undammed, he to recount events of the voyage and I to relate, with appropriate gestures such as the smacking of palm to brow, the details of several household crises so deplorable that he either did not notice, or forbore to comment upon, the changes I had wrought.

At last we retired to bed and I to the first carefree sleep I had known for some time, for it had been a strain having no one to help me "listen" at night in the vast upper floor of the ancient villa, the listening being a semi-waking state maintained in case some of the numerous roving thieves then operating in the Italian countryside should be trying to get into our sanctuary and rifle our hard-won supplies (to mention the least sinister of their probable objectives). Tonight, at least, Frank could do the listening. I intended to sleep.

Those six weeks away from the hazards of post-war suburban Rome, however, must have anaesthetized Frank's listening sense. In any case it was not he who rose up at two a.m., alerted by a slight ripping sound which registered at once in my mind as a corner of the studio door shutters being pried up. It was I who tripped barefoot across the floor and peered out the crack in the French doors and saw, almost directly below me, the figure of a man who was indeed operating on the shutters. I ran to the bed and laid clammy hands on the shoulders of my snoring husband, and dragged him forth to see what was going on. Instinctively he reached for the gun which had always been kept, at night, in his shoe under the edge of the bed. Not there. In the desk drawer, then, where it was locked during the day. He groped for the desk and came up against the alien bureau instead.

"Where in hell is the gun?" he hissed in the darkness.

"In...in the desk," I hissed back rather feebly.

"And what in God's name have you done with the *desk?*" But he did not wait for my reply and stumbled gun-less to the doors to see what he could see. There was the intruder, still prying at the shutter, a dandy target in pot-shot range. As we watched (I more in terror of the inevitable reckoning with my enraged spouse than of what the fellow below might do), we saw him leave the studio door and walk in a leisurely fashion out under the archway.

Beyond the arch was the door to the garage, not visible to us from our bedroom. In the garage was the jeep, but with the kind of foresight the circumstances of those unsettled days engendered, Frank had thoughtfully removed its wheels and stored them in the house before he left on his trip. We had no particular anxiety about the jeep except that a theoretical accomplice, prying elsewhere about the house, might have already gained entrance to the ground floor and got at the wheels. The matter had to be investigated without delay.

Pressing the bell for Bandini, whose chief duty was the keeping of a wary ear out at night, but who evidently on this occasion had his wary ear amply swathed in bedclothes, Frank pulled on his pants and went to the other side of the second floor to retrieve the gun before going downstairs. Bandini met him, likewise in the pants-pulling-on stage, and likewise with a gun. I heard them tactfully identifying themselves to each other in the darkness.

Yes, Bandini and his wife had heard certain sounds. Bandini was, in fact, just on the point of getting up to investigate when our bell gave him the necessary impetus. His wife crouched in her bed and I returned to mine while our two brave men went forth to search the terrain.

The garage door, they found, was broken open. The jeep within still sat on its blocks. The obvious conclusion was that, having broken into the garage and found the jeep wheels missing, the vandal had assumed, correctly, that the wheels must be inside the house. Why he gave up his attempt to reach them via the studio when no sound had warned him that he was observed we could only conjecture, unless with true Italian efficiency he had to go back for a tool.

At any rate, our man had escaped into the surrounding gloom of the wheat fields and hedgerows, or possibly even into the neighboring peasant houses, and nothing had been stolen *this* time. Nevertheless, everybody was in a high state of moral indignation that another attempt had been made to breach our fortress.

"I could have got him easy," Frank said belligerently, "if you hadn't been inspired to move the furniture on *this* day of all days."

Housebreakings and barnyard thievery were then so common in the countryside that shots rang out nightly in the dark from one quarter or another, and those of us unfortunate enough to be paying fantastic rents for places in which to live naturally shared a fine sense of outrage over the continual depredations. It was no time for me to voice my secret conviction that maybe it was just as well Frank hadn't had the gun. I didn't relish the idea of a shot burglar writhing in our courtyard, even though I had to admit it would have been a pleasure to have scared the living daylights out of him.

So for the succeeding weeks I kept my mouth discreetly shut and my head hung at an appropriately humble angle. And of course, whenever we had occasion thereafter to relate the events of the Night the Jeep was Almost Stolen, the little matter of my having moved the furniture was always the punch line of the story. It was a long time before I could so much as move an ottoman without a guilty feeling.

The stigma of this occasion was finally removed from my person, oddly enough, only because of another furniture moving episode which proved notably advantageous and to my everlasting credit in the eyes of my husband.

The jeep, which was a borrowed one, was returned to its owner when he came back to Rome from an assignment elsewhere. We were carless until, answering an ad in a Rome daily paper, Frank came upon the dismembered body of a lovely little Lancia that its owner, lately a prisoner of war in Africa for several years, was eager to liquidate. Its parts, deviously scattered to thwart commandeering by the erstwhile German authorities, could be reassembled and it would be as good as new.

Frank had come home drooling over his find, a cream-colored, custom-built job with red leather upholstery. The mental picture I conjured up from his glowing description did not exactly fit the reality, I must say, for though the details were approximately accurate, nothing had quite prepared me for the fact that the car had obviously been custom built for midgets. You could sit in the rear seat if you sat at an angle and with your chin resting on your knees, a position I myself was not able to assume with any degree of comfort. Still, it was a car, and cars were not easily come by in those days in Italy.

After the kind of tedious and hilarious negotiations which inevitably accompany any such deal as the purchase of a motor car, this fey contraption was finally ours. From then on we slept, if it can be dignified by the term, with one ear hung from the balcony in the direction of the garage where this priceless jewel was housed. But the garage was just too far away and too vulnerable. It was across the moat, as it were. Obviously, it was impractical to take the wheels off every night. Obviously, too, it was impossible not to visualize some brutal *Romano* making off with this delectable Sabine *macchina*. The two facts cancelled out anything so trivial as sleep.

Preoccupation with the safety of our precious car became a family state of mind that summer. The sprawling old villa had plenty of waste space. Surely somewhere inside the fortress we ought to be able to find a niche for the Lancia. There was only the quite elementary problem of getting it in.

Just inside the archway was the so-called studio, a great bare room of about forty by forty feet that gave onto the courtyard with a glass door in a huge panel of windows. The studio floor was of tile laid right on the earth, and the door sill was no more than four inches—a brick's width—high. We used to come into this practically unused and skimpily furnished room and gaze speculatively about. But the door was only of normal door size set among the glass panels. If there were only some way to open up another panel! However, short of remodeling the whole wall, it couldn't be done.

In addition to the studio on the ground floor of the villa there were: a big dining room, a solarium (where the sun never came), an unused bedroom, a couple of store-rooms, an "office," an enormous kitchen and laundry, and the entrance hall which was about twice the size of a normal, modern living room. There was also the caretaker's room which, with the kitchen, constituted the only portion of this floor that might be said to be fully utilized. The rest was an ostentatious spread of space that inevitably set us to brooding on the possibilities of getting Sabina somehow under our own roof.

Probably the room affording the best grounds for speculation in this direction should have been the entrance hall, since it, like the studio, opened directly onto the courtyard with only a narrow terrace between. But it had obviously been the *padrone*'s favorite sitting room and into it he had put all the oddments of furniture and bric-a-brac that his collector's propensities had caused him to assemble over the years, and moreover, when you are thinking about a place to park a car it doesn't normally come to mind that it could be sandwiched between a fireplace, complete with Staffordshire dogs, on one side, and a refectory table surmounted by French oil lamps with fluted glass shades on the other. An Epsteinian stone Madonna clutching an amorphous infant glowered down from above the mantelpiece and a large, wormy, wooden Madonna defended the door. Ivory-colored, red-printed chintz framed the windows and glass panels of the entrance. As in most Italian interiors the light was dim, for the fixtures all held ten-watt bulbs, and in the daytime the curtains were drawn to protect the colors of the rugs. The facts of peeling paint on the woodwork and leprous splotches on the wallpaper were thus subordinated to the rather lovely blending of colors.

The high ceiling of the entrance hall was supported by four pillars, widely spaced. The doors to the hallway and to the stairs were arched, and there were arched open niches flanking the doors which contained vases of artificial flowers under bell-jars (smaller and less offensive than their attic counterparts, and somehow suitable to the general décor).

It was actually a charming room, but at this point in our tenancy of the house charm was a minor consideration. I would have been prepared to sacrifice even this to the prosaic necessity for getting some sleep at night if the idea had occurred to me.

I remember I was standing by the door that morning trying to decide whether it was worth while going out onto the terrace and stretching out in the deck chair, since Maria would be sure to shake the dust-cloth on me from the window above, when I noticed something about the door I hadn't observed before. Maybe more paint had chipped off, or maybe my eyes were brighter than usual. At all events, I discerned what looked like a hinge on what I had hitherto assumed to be stationary glass panels on either side of the door. I bent down and chipped away a little more of the six or eight layers of paint with my fingernail and lo and behold, there it was—a hinge! And on the other panel, too. The full three panels could be opened. What a discovery!

I turned to the room itself and it took my skilled rearranger's brain about ten seconds to solve the problem. Everything between the two center pillars must go. Wing chairs with attendant wrought-iron lamps would be fine by the upstairs fireplace. The oval table would do in the hall. We needed some additional furniture—didn't we?— in the big bare studio. I called Bandini and Maria without a second's hesitation and didn't even bother to explain my sudden brainstorm except to say *"C'e troppo roba qui,"* there's too much stuff here.

When we had finished, the entrance hall had a denuded aspect which Frank was sure to notice when he came home. I looked forward to his coming, to his bridling cognizance that *something* had been *moved*. Meanwhile I set Bandini to chipping away the paint from the ancient slide catches and removing a nail or two from the door frame, and together we opened the panels and sent generations of spiders scurrying around the doorjamb.

"Che bell' aria!" I cried, inhaling deeply when all the panels stood wide, as if I had been suffocating previously with only one door and a couple of windows open. Bandini looked at me strangely, but I expect he laid it to my *stato interessante*. If anyone gave the order to put the car into the parlor it was not going to be me. That touch of lunacy could originate with the master of the house.

Frank, when he came home, reacted according to plan. "What are you trying to do to *this* room?" he wanted to know.

"Don't you like it?" I asked innocently, enjoying my moment of triumph.

"It looks bare..." he began. Then I saw his eye begin to measure the space between the pillars. I saw him begin mentally to roll up the rugs.

Taking his hand in mine, I led him to the door, drew back the curtains, and pointed to the now fully revealed hinges.

"By God," he said, putting his arm tenderly about me, "by God, you're a genius!" And then he sprang the trap that marked him forever as another crazy *Americano*.

"Bandini," he bellowed, "hey, Bandini! *Mettiamo qui la macchina!*"

Bandini came in with a shocked look on his face. "*Signore—la macchina!*" he cried incredulously, and he began striding about the room and out onto the terrace, and he came back and made certain gestures with his hands which anybody could see meant that a couple of little wooden ramps were needed to facilitate the approach to the terrace, a matter of about eight inches.

Frank said "*bene*," and Bandini hurried away to get his saw and hammer.

We waited until after dark to bring the car in that first night, just in case the neighbors might be looking. Maria and Bandini and I stood around holding our breath, fully expecting that Frank would drive right on through the far wall and into the sunless solarium, or hit a pillar, or at least upset the wormy Madonna, but he came in as gently as a settling gull and stopped in front of the fireplace.

Bandini inspected the floor minutely for tire marks but there were none. Maria got down on her hands and knees and peered underneath to see if anything was leaking. Bandini went out and brought in the ramps and then clanged down the iron door across the entrance. Gathered inside in the dim light of the ten-watt bulbs, we shook hands solemnly and Frank reached into the liquor cabinet which stood in the latitude of the gas tank and took out four little glasses and a *liquore*. We drank to *buon riposo*, and then we all burst out laughing and went to bed.

For a time Frank got up early mornings and put the car out, and brought it in after dark at night. Then we got bolder and made our exits and entrances in broad daylight, but that was after we were satisfied that Sabina was fully housebroken, that she neither dripped oil nor caved in the tile, and the *padrone* could have no reasonable grounds for complaint, should the word get abroad, except possibly that a certain indignity had been committed. And every night, with the Lancia safely bedded, as we hauled in the ramps and clanged down the iron door, we all enjoyed a pleasant conspiratorial moment and the comforting thought that nobody could steal her now.

We all began to lose our haggard expressions, and I am glad to say there have never been further recriminations in our household whenever I have taken it into my whimsical head to improve (shall we say?) on the arrangement of a room.

As a matter of fact, my husband tends to regard my furniture moving now with a certain superstitious awe. It almost certainly saved Sabina, for whom (or for which) he had an inordinate passion, from a cruel fate. And in an expansive mood recently Frank confided, regarding that earlier fiasco, that he had always been secretly glad he hadn't been able to lay his hands on the gun that night.

"You never know what you'll do in a moment like that," he said solemnly. "I might even have *killed* the guy. Or wounded him, which in Italy can be even worse—having him survive to sue you for damages." He spent the next ten minutes expanding the grim picture of himself in the clutches of Italian legal machinery, languishing interminably in the arms of Regina Coeli which is not, as might be supposed, some heavenly sanctuary or even one of the five hundred churches, but the grim old Roman jail.

"God!" Frank concluded, mopping his brow. His tone was not only not irreverent, but carried the quite obvious implication that my furniture shifting elbow, at least upon certain occasions, has unmistakably been divinely joggled.

2

The Fifth Wind Was Blowing? Case Dismissed...

History was a long time maturing (and with a certain grim irony) the circumstances which should bring together a congenital shifter of furniture and a place that was unexcelled as a theater of operations. Never was there a house that offered more mouth-watering possibilities in the line of rearrangement, or for that matter, never was there a house with more lurid potentialities for murder, intrigue, robbery—and even for elegant and restful living, when times were right, which was practically never—than that Roman villa, that monstrosity of brick and stone which came to be known in the course of time as the house that haunted us.

It was called the House of the Four Winds—*Villa dei Quattro Venti*—but that was an understatement. We lived there, or rather carried on a caricature of domestic tranquility within its rambling confines, for two years, so we came to be well versed in the prevailing climate of the place. And while the usual four winds consulted by mariners and fishermen each blew upon us in its season, there was yet an eerie, unorthodox, and strictly local fifth wind that seemed to bear no relationship to the accepted variants of the original four.

This wind came unexpectedly in winter. It came on days when the house was impossibly dank and cold, a cold that hung like a tangible curtain in the doorways, lay like an invisible frigid pool on the stone floors. It would be on those days when you had had more than the normal amount of travail getting the fires started in the fireplace and the tile stoves, just when you had risen from in front of the last grate with soot on your face, out of breath from administering artificial respiration into the stove mouth, just as you were dusting off your soot-stained hands and saying, "There, I guess it will go now"—the very idea of a fire making you feel a little warmer, and you listened with satisfaction to the flames snapping away at the wood.

And that was the moment the fifth wind arrived. You knew it had come because the snapping suddenly ceased and smoke began to seep out the front of the stove, and in frantic haste to save your precious fire you opened the stove door only to have smoke and soot and sparks come pouring out into your face.

It was not just a momentary down draft, it was a good steady current of wind and it came directly down the chimneys and you could feel it fanning out into the room. It was unexplainable and it was contrary to nature, but there it was, and there remained no alternative but to get the smoldering wood out of the stove as quickly as possible and dump it outdoors. It was then, with the doors and windows all open, that you discovered that it was warm outside. The dank midwinter cold had vanished.

So that was the fifth wind, and maybe it was really the *sirocco*, for like the *sirocco* it was perceived less as a directional wind than a pressure of air, a heaviness of the atmosphere, a state of mind, a malignancy of the spirit which came as a disturbing influence in the household, passing on before the warmth it generated could penetrate the stone-cold rooms, so that while the stoves refused to draw you had to flee outdoors for warmth, leaving your work, your unfinished projects, and giving in to an invisible natural force of disruption, a thing with a certain charm of its own which nevertheless, like so many things in that charming land, was actually a sort of chronic affliction.

They say that crimes of passion committed while the *sirocco* blows are excusable. I can only hope for similar clemency for whatever breaches of the local mores, unreasonablenesses, and arrogances I may have committed in that house of the fifth wind.

3

All the Comforts of Rome

My first glimpse of the *Villa dei Quattro Venti* came at the end of a five-hour, nonstop jeep ride from Naples, and in my by then extremis about getting to the bathroom, I was in no condition to take in details.

We had hurtled violently up the coast road through mangled and prostrate villages, bearing on their few standing facades the unhealed pock-marks of mankind's most loathsome malady. It was June of 1946, the first spring after the war. Behind me lay months of tedious preparations, getting myself and my young daughter, Marta, outfitted—physically and mentally—for life on a different continent. (And don't think the mental hazard is minor in the case of a six-year-old to whom Father is a pleasant myth, the neighborhood gang is far more important than mere parents, and the block you grew up on is the center of the universe.)

Behind me lay a trip across America with six trunks and ten pieces of hand luggage undertaken at the moment when porters as well as railway trainmen were on strike so that we progressed from station to station with about as much assurance of reaching our destination on time as Lewis and Clark had of getting over the Rockies by snowfall.

Behind me lay ten days at sea aboard the barely converted troop transport, the *Marine Carp*, with as odd an assortment of characters as you would find outside of a zoo, including the psychopathic lady whose husband was taking her back to visit relatives in the Old Country in hopes of effecting a cure.

To add to my general confusion, my landlubber's head still carried the imprint of waves. And now came a kaleidoscope of dusty ruins where bougainvillea flung its improbable cerise banners across broken pink walls; of geraniums red and Mediterranean blue; of scrawny, squawking chickens flapping out of our way and scrawny, shave-topped children trying to impede it.

We had been impelled to such haste by the well-documented belief that to pause momentarily on an Italian highway in those days was to invite being hijacked and relieved of one's hard-come-by possessions. They were the days when bridges under construction were carted bodily away at night. When a jeep driver leaning against the rear of his jeep to enjoy a cigarette might suddenly find himself sprawled in the road, his prop having been driven away from in front of him.

Yes, there was ample reason for not loitering along the way, but it was an experience which gave me a permanent antipathy to jeeps and a somewhat confused first impression of the house that was to be our home, for better or for worse, during the next two years.

If you had grown up, as I did, in the far and middle West and you were suddenly informed that you were to live in a villa in the country on the outskirts of Rome, you would probably have as little basis as I had for visualizing said villa. If you were told it had impressive hedgerows, a large garden, and a swimming pool, you would probably imagine something Hollywoodian. At least you would patch together some concepts of the country places of local cattle barons, or of chewing gum magnates outside Chicago. It had to be something pretty fancy, by any previously existing standards. Rolling lawns, I pictured, formal gardens...

But rushing madly up that coastal road in the early summer drought, in the wind-swept rear end of a jeep and peering out into the barren countryside as it flew by, I found nothing to contribute to my vision of *the* villa. I could only hope that Rome was greener, more watered, less desolate. Marta, beside me, gazed steadily into the wind with a sort of entranced expression. Behind us an army truck thundered in our wake bearing our possessions.

As we ticked off village after village I began to think Italy was probably all like this—just broken walls, glaring piazzas, miserable people, and a general tone of dust and despair. Was there no end to this war-blazed road? Frank kept encouraging me by saying we were *almost* there now, if that can be termed encouragement when each hopefully approached village in turn receded behind us and the road stretched on ahead relentlessly.

I gave up hope entirely at Albano. It had looked so promising as we approached that I had been sure it was the Eternal—but eternally deferred—city which was our objective. *Only* another twenty miles! I went into such a decline of morale, what with five hours on the rack of a jeep with neither food nor comfort station, that I stopped looking at the scenery until somebody said we were turning into our driveway.

Our driveway! It was a broken down arch of brick with barbed wire fences stretching, or rather reclining, to either side of it. We bumped up a dusty road through denuded fields toward an indistinguishable huddle of buildings graced by a few tormented fruit trees. Was *that* the place Frank had written me about in such glowing terms? I gave him a sidelong glance, just checking whether anything had happened to his head during the years of his absence. His profile was noncommittal. Still, I didn't much care at the moment what sort of place we were coming to, just so it had a bathroom, or at least a path out back. We paused at a gate under an archway, then entered an enclosed yard.

"Show the *Signora* to the *gabinetto*," Frank said to the little daughter of the custodians the moment she opened the front door. There was a slight preliminary formality. The custodian's wife, a squat, youngish woman with a pleasantly ugly face, had to be greeted. My rudimentary Italian had to be called into its first hesitant use for the exchange of obsequies, and we were off. I followed the short white frock, the short black curls and the sturdy brown legs up the staircase, around two landings and across an unbelievable expanse of somberly gleaming red tile floor.

"*Ecco, Signora,*" said the little girl at last with a suggestion of a curtsey as she opened the door for me. I thanked the child and entered the blue-blond vastness of the bathroom. My faculties returned, and my observations began there.

Well, I have seen bathrooms and bathrooms, large ones and small ones, but this was the first I had seen that would dwarf the living room of a tract home. Its *gabinetto* was cozily recessed at the end of an enormous blond wardrobe which occupied one long wall. A nine-foot window lighted up the gleaming white and blue tiles. There was a pear-shaped porcelain object in one angle which I was to learn is a standard fixture in European bathrooms. At the moment I did not even know what it was called, so I did what all greenhorns do, I tried its various spigots. But what was that foot pedal thing underneath? I stepped on it to find out, and was rewarded by a stream of water shooting up into my gaping face.

And there was the bath department, the tub installed on a dais with an elaborate instrument panel above it for regulating temperatures, angles, and pressures. That dangling cord over the tub? I reached to try it, but remembering my experience with the bidet, I drew back my hand. I didn't want any unexpected stream of water hitting me from above. But it was, on closer inspection, obviously a bell-pull and for a moment I was lost in delightful speculation as to just what must be expected of the *Signora* in her bath—or, unnerving thought, did the *Signore* use it too? Did the maid come trotting in to wash *his* back? I began to think it was no place for a simple girl from Chicago and points west.

In this timorous frame of mind I emerged from the bathroom and found myself in the—what is this, the *living room* on the second floor? I had passed through it, of course, en route to the bathroom, but I had not really seen it in my preoccupation with more elemental things. Now I saw it for the first time and I had to sit down quickly in the nearest chair to take in the details.

It was truly a lovely room. There was an expansive stillness and a palette blending of colors that merged into an inexpressible emotion. Something remembered, something desired, something completed. The draperies moved in the afternoon breeze. The shuttered sunlight latticed the dark red, irregular paving block floor. Overhead—but high—the dark, rough-hewn ancient beams were a shadowy acreage. An indefinable fragrance from great bowls of pearly white oleander blossoms mingled with the faint smoky smell of the empty fireplace and the sweet, arid, pine-touched breath of Roman summer. It smelled like home, like a clean, lived-in, tended place where more, much more than oil and wax and water had gone into the luster of its surfaces, the glint of its antique windowpanes. It spoke, on that drowsy summer afternoon, of Christmases past, of First Communions, of Easter cleanings, of candle and fire-light and spring blossoms.

I had always fancied an upstairs living room and here my dreams were rather more than amply fulfilled. The room stretched across the breadth of the house with windows to south and north. It was a room that was to come to seem smaller as time went on, but even intimacy could not diminish it beyond the more than forty feet of its length, the twenty-five of its width or the twenty of its height. At the moment it served to banish my qualms about the state of my husband's judgment.

I saw that I was surrounded by antiques, tables of rare and lovely woods properly riddled by worms. Vases of majolica elaborately decorated with serpentine heads and human breasts; urns of marble and lamp bases of alabaster (an odd lumping of furniture down the center of the room—let's see, *this* table could go *there*...); busts of bronze. Gilt framed paintings dark with age. Old maps, old prints. Vast rugs from the Orient honorably threadbare. Gilded clocks and sprays of artificial flowers under bell jars. Carved and massive wardrobes that must have been built or assembled in this room since no door could have accommodated them.

The mantelpiece of the fireplace was above my head, and mounted below it, like a coat of arms, was an elaborately carved wooden plaque which, upon inspection, proved to be the keyhole piece from some massive ancient door. Looking into that king-sized keyhole, I felt a little like Alice, and wondered how I should find my way out of this strange place without falling down a rabbit hole, wading through a pool of my own tears or at least blundering into the bedroom of some austere old countess. I had no proprietary sense at the moment, no assurance that whatever I wandered into here would be my own territory by virtue of a laboriously arrived-at and meticulously detailed contract, plus a shocking monetary deposit totally unjustified by our modest means but cheerfully surrendered in view of the fact that here, after five years of wartime separation, was to be our first real home. (And also in view of the fact that anything less expensive was not to be had at that period in Rome unless one had advantageous connections with the still-existing military government.)

But as luck would have it, the first door I came to was to the stairway and so I descended to the even more confusing if more prosaic reality of the mountain of trunks, bags, and boxes which had been dumped unceremoniously into the center of the reception hall. My elusive husband was escaping out the front door. "Hey, wait!" I cried. "Don't leave me here alone!"

"You are not alone," he said sternly. "You have the woman here. This truck driver is a prisoner of war and I have to get him back to town by five." I stared in amazement at the fellow climbing up into the truck. It was my first and only encounter with a member of the erstwhile master race, and I certainly had not expected to find him an apple-cheeked boy in shorts.

Everything was very confusing. This house, for instance, that looked as we approached it like an abandoned cannery, was a palace within.

But wait a minute—maybe it wasn't so terrible on the outside as I had thought at first. I had followed Frank out onto the terrace and now I could get a better look at the house. The lowering sun had taken the white glare off the courtyard and flung graceful shadows across it. The house glowed warm red-brown and rose with lattices of palest green. It had an old and weathered and mellow look, and I felt the gears meshing in my provincial brain as my preconceived notions about country places went into reverse.

Here was a house that had dozed for centuries in the Italian sunshine, had endured, season after season, the torrential rains which rob its surrounding acres of their topsoil and turn the ancient Tiber turgid as gray poster paint. Hand-hewn beams and balconies had been toasting and browning and warping. Roof tiles had been growing loose and lichenous. Arbors had become dank tunnels of matted leaves and gnarled webs of branches supported on rotting trellises which leaned ever nearer the earth.

Had it been, in its fine strong heyday, the big house of some vast estate? Had it been a *pensione*, a *trattoria*, and, as some said, a house of assignation? We could not piece together from the neighbors its story. Certainly it had passed from *padrone* to *padrone* over the years, but it was the kind of house that nobody particularly noticed amid the more modern, more pretentious villas that surrounded it on the Roman highlands. It was not a famous villa. No flamboyant Roman emperors had ever chosen its site for their spectacular abodes, no historic ruins underlay it. It was just a great, square, barn-like stone structure that had probably been falling to ruin when a big Roman industrialist picked it up for the proverbial song, moved the chickens out of the attic, the goats out of the bedrooms, knocked it into habitable shape and resold it to the man from whom, in a moment of mixed good and bad fortune, we eventually leased it.

The place had been added to and taken from over the years. It had been extended here and closed off there. Accretions of peasant houses issued from the back of it with shelving, irregular roofs. It had been modernized with electricity and a central heating system, and with gas which usurped the function of the enormous black iron range with double fireboxes which still monopolized one wall of the kitchen. But the modernization was a thing of decades past. The central heating system no longer functioned. The electricity was a complicated web-work of inadequate wiring, hidden fuses, divided currents which defied either amateur tinkering or professional research. The water system was antiquated and complex. The gas was whimsical.

Yet there it stood, the house, and still stands, its twenty-odd rooms and nooks and crannies, sealed-off pantries and subterranean ways—its whole staunch, squat, amorphous structure, all resisting patiently in the Italian manner both disintegration and improvement, acquiring, at its long leisure, the smell of mildew and of sunshine and the look of a house that was—and is—more than any of the modern villas which surround it, an integral and authentic part of its landscape.

Of its assets I was becoming pleasantly aware, that first afternoon as the sun slipped down behind the umbrella pines and sculptured cypresses that graced our western horizon. Of its shortcomings I was as yet happily ignorant. For the moment I was very hungry and my maternal instincts reasserted themselves to the extent of wondering what had become of my missing child who, so far as I knew, had still not been introduced to the interior of the house and, specifically, the *gabinetto*. Nor had she been hungry on the trip, nor tired. And to my repeated entreaties en-route, "Don't *you* have to stop?" she had always cheerfully replied in the negative. Little monster!

4

We, Of Course, Are All Gentlemen Here

In America a man may contract marriage, adopt a child, dispose of his property to his heirs forever with much less formality than is required in Italy for the simple matter of renting a house or apartment.

If, in my first hours at the House of the Four Winds, I had no sense of being the *padrona*, it was largely because I had not yet heard from my husband the story of the signing of the lease which he, aided and abetted by sundry lawyers, assistants, and advisers, had negotiated during the months preceding my arrival in Italy.

Frank and I had been separated a long time by the war. When he departed from Chicago in the spring of 1940 our baby, Marta, was three months old. When he returned, she could read and write, draw very cleverly, and was an old hand at extracting nickels and dimes almost painlessly from the parental pocketbook. This all represented no unusual precocity on the part of our offspring. The simple fact was that she had reached school age during his absence.

Nor was this the end of our trial by separation. After a brief vacation in the States, Frank was reassigned to Rome, and went back to Italy in November 1945, on a Liberty ship along with a good many tons of American wheat.

Our eventual reunion in Rome was conditional upon Frank's finding and renting a suitable place for us to live, a condition which proved almost insurmountable in view of the Italian genius for complicating situations.

The owner of many a villa in Italy in those days did not have one lira to rub against another, and any American with even a modest salary by American standards was a very welcome sight. One might have thought, under the circumstances, that the matter of renting a house would have been made easy—nay, pleasant. On the contrary. No mere question of imminent starvation can deprive a Roman of the rites and ceremonies attendant upon executing a contract. And in this case the owner and his staff of attorneys seemed determined to extract the last full measure of delight from the process.

In the beginning there were two to bear the brunt of the contractual battle. Another American family was to have shared the villa with us, so Frank and George were engaged jointly in lining up a habitation for their respective families. As it turned out, George was recalled to the States before his family was able to join him in Italy, and we inherited the villa, its costs and problems.

The hour for the contract signing was set by the owner, and the two Americans appeared at the appointed time prepared to kiss off the signing of the lease and move into the villa in a matter of hours. Little did they know at the moment that it was to be a protracted series of conferences the like of which was not seen again until the nations of the world huddled at Geneva over the problems of Indochina, and with almost as little hope of eventual success.

It began on a basis of mutual deference with the pouring of several rounds of liqueurs. The landlord, a small, dapper and perfumed gentleman with impeccable clothes and precisely parted hair, was flanked by his *avvocato*, a formidable figure that would have been paunchy if times had been more favorable, but in the austere period they had just passed through, Roman lawyers like Roman cats and Roman horses and Romans in general were still on the gaunt side. He, like his retainer, however, was tailored to perfection and not a hair was out of place.

The severity of the contract which was unveiled after the pouring of libations may have been inspired in part by the sartorial contrast provided by our team of Americans. War correspondents as a breed are the despair of the army. With all of a captain's privileges and none of the responsibilities and discipline, they are inclined to wear the uniform with an air of rakishness, to say the  least. The cap that Maria ceremoniously took from Frank's hands as he entered, for example, was an object of international reputation. He had repulsed various offers for it from envious young men who lack his capacity to give a garment that lived-in look. Word got about that Correspondent Brutto had worn that same cap in every landing from Okinawa to Normandy, though the truth was he had been most of the time in Switzerland in mufti and had had barely six months to imbue his uniform with that distinctive appearance of service above and beyond the call of duty.

George, on the other hand, was a man with a passion for changing his shirt and running up cleaners' bills, but with his spectacles, his rumpled and thinning hair, and his absentmindedness, he was likely to appear in "pink" trousers combined with an Eisenhower jacket. The fact that he changed his underwear every day was almost sure to be lost on Italians, whose respect for a uniform is notorious and whose sensibilities are outraged by such casualness. It is highly probable that the cause of these Americans as potential tenants of the villa was  considerably weakened by their lack of attention to a *bella figura*. How could you trust a man to keep an orderly house who clumped across the marble floor in paratrooper's boots?

Still, the atmosphere was one of the most formal courtesy, and the *avvocato*, in a sonorous voice, began reading the contract paragraph by paragraph. With growing sentiments of alarm the Americans listened and scanned the ten-page inventory of the items in the house that were about to pass into their safekeeping, complete to the last clay flowerpot in the garage. In value they totaled up to thousands of dollars. Amid the verbiage of the contract, moreover, Frank and George discerned the unsettling information that their responsibility for the house and its contents did not cease with what we think of as "reasonable care," but even if the house were forcibly entered and robbed, or if it were gutted by fire from whatever cause, they, the tenants, were fully responsible and would be obliged to reimburse the owner who, naturally, carried no insurance.

The prospective tenants, being poor but practical men, immediately envisioned here an eventuality that could leave them in a very embarrassing situation indeed. An eventuality which, however, could scarcely be mentioned with delicacy and without shattering the atmosphere of gentility that surrounded all the characters in the drama—namely, the hypothetical case of a landlord arranging a robbery or a fire for the purpose of collecting cash value from his tenants.

Clearly the would-be tenants required legal advice. With the plea of needing to give detailed study to the lease, the first meeting was adjourned with handshaking all around and fervent abjurations to remain in good health and to convene again soon.

Was it purely coincidental that the lawyer with whom they consulted, out of the five thousand lawyers in Rome, should have turned out to be a friend of the landlord's attorney? At any rate this genial character who accompanied them to the next meeting advised that such a clause was routine and it was quite unthinkable that it had been inserted for any nefarious purpose. The landlord must, of course, protect himself against an unscrupulous tenant as well, one who, if bound only by the "reasonable care" theory might himself arrange a robbery for his own advantage.

"We are speaking, of course, in hypothetical terms," the attorney explained, "since we, naturally, are all gentlemen here."

So, for the moment, they abandoned their efforts to have the terms of responsibility lightened. But there was another clause that caught the attention of the Americans and seemed to cast some doubt upon the oft-repeated assertion that all those involved in signing this particular lease were indeed gentlemen. The lessees were to bind themselves to a strictly moral way of life which precluded the inviting of women to the house for any purpose whatsoever. So severe was the wording of the clause that Frank and George had some momentary doubts about being able to bring their wives there when they should arrive. As the contract stood, they would be in shocking violation of it if they undertook to entertain the local chapter of the W.C.T.U.. A cocktail party or an intimate dinner for friends of their grandmothers would have put them in jeopardy of eviction and heavy fines.

"What do they take us for?" Frank said to George, and George said, "From what I hear, the landlord himself is not one who should be levying moral restrictions on anybody. We won't sign it unless they eliminate that clause."

This obdurate attitude upon which, united, they stood, threw the landlord into such a state of confusion that the deadlocked meeting was adjourned until another day when he returned flanked by *two* lawyers, the second one English-speaking. "This clause," he pointed out, "is merely a normal precaution against a purely hypothetical situation."

"The persons signing this particular contract for this particular house and expected to pay this spectacular amount of rent are not, however, hypothetical persons," Frank pointed out. "They are actual persons. We, as the actual signers of this lease, resent the implication that we are not men of good moral character, and we refuse to sign unless the clause is deleted." George, wearing his best expression of moral indignation, struck his fist in his palm and managed to convey an impressive picture of a united front. The landlord and his attorneys withdrew to another room for a long private conference, from which they eventually emerged prepared to accede to the demands of the prospective tenants, on this point.

This had been a concession of such magnitude, however, that they refused to budge on any other controversial points, including that which bound the lessee to retain the custodian and his family as fixtures in the house—a situation which Frank and George had accurately foreseen as a potential cause of friction.

Three weeks had dragged by in haggling over the lease, but at last the two Americans emerged triumphant but financially depleted with the keys to the mansion. Some time after they had taken possession of the house, one of George's Italian cousins, himself a lawyer, came to call. George showed him the contract. The lawyer read it through with growing expressions of alarm, clapping his hand to his forehead dramatically at the end of almost every paragraph.

"What have you signed here?" he cried. "This is extremely irregular!" He offered to take the contract and work it over sensibly and bring the landlord to task for its original unsuitability.

After several more weeks of negotiations between the respective lawyers and the owner, George's cousin returned with the contract modified to his satisfaction. It is possible that George and Frank affixed their signatures to this new document in a somewhat absentminded manner, for by this time they were involved in the almost equally complicated problem of arranging transportation from America for their families.

The ink was scarcely dry on their signatures, when George received his orders to return to the States. It was a grave blow for them both, and Frank would gladly have given up the whole proposition by this time but there was no way out. The contract was binding and a gentleman—even a hypothetical gentleman—sticks by his obligations, especially when his life's savings are invested therein.

5

She Made Her Own Bed

For a time it seemed that a great friendship was on the point of blossoming between Maria and me. For practically the whole of the first week we regarded each other with a certain delicacy and tenderness, and I overheard her describing me to some friends in the kitchen as very *gentile*, and very *carina*, even as a "real lady," if I did not mistake the meaning of *proprio una Signora*. Not in my memory had anyone used such adjectives in assessing my virtues and it generated a fine respect for Maria's keen judgment of character.

I suppose it was a certain fatigue and confusion resulting from the journey and the newness—or oldness—of everything that accounted for my temporary lack of stamina, but I confess I found Maria's estimate of me a pleasant change from the way I had always been sized up by friends and relatives alike as "competent," "efficient," "determined" (which all boil down in less polite terms to "hard headed").

Moreover, Maria (who was actually French rather than Italian and quite snooty about it) was concerned that I not be bored in my new surroundings. She questioned Frank minutely to determine the state of my morale; she even offered to take me for walks around the countryside and the village to brighten me up if I were downcast. This, too, was a novelty. My husband, who might reasonably have been expected to concern himself over my fluctuations of temperament, was at the moment much more concerned over Maria's. "The woman has been knocking herself out getting ready for you," he said. "Why don't you see what you can do to help her out with the work."

And of course that was just what I had had in mind doing. Not having been informed from the beginning that there were any domestic servants involved in this situation, I had come prepared to run my household on a business-as-usual basis. Cooking? Of course I would do the cooking. Sweep and dust and iron? Naturally, what else had I been doing up to now except for some frivolous sidelines like photography and horses. (I was going to have lots of time on my hands for the housework here, what with no hay to fork down from the mow and no stalls to clean.)

But you can't blame a girl for luxuriating in that cherished feeling as long as possible. There was a certain other-worldliness about my first days at the villa. It began, I remember, the moment the jeep disappeared out of the gateway and I was left alone to my new responsibilities. I was feeling very inadequate to the situation, indeed. Very alone. I didn't even know where my child had vanished to or whether she had been whisked off to some den of iniquity even more lurid than her own natural instincts might have led her to.

I was standing on the terrace wondering what to do first when a masculine voice boomed behind me and I turned to see, not some dark-browed Italian male as I had expected, but the squat person of the custodian's wife. "The little one," she said, speaking in Italian but accompanying her words with such vivid pantomime that her meaning was perfectly clear, "is outside playing with my daughter, Rita."

This was news that I found very comforting as it tended to bear out what I had been monotonously repeating to deaf young ears up to now, namely that it is possible to have fun even in a foreign country. I gave up the project of looking for Marta to bring her in to be washed and fed. Better to let nature take its course, I decided.

I followed the woman back into the house and together we approached the mountain of trunks and bags. "If you will indicate which you require," she said, "I will carry your valises to your room."

It was the first intimation I had had that the custodian's wife served also as a maid. I had thought that she and her husband were in the nature of gatekeepers, but now I saw that she expected to wait on me. I pointed out the most essential bags and she picked them up, but when I too attempted to carry one her "*No, no Signora! Faccio io, faccio io!*" shook the rafters. Remembering the way I had shouldered three cases at a time on every station platform across America, this struck me as slightly overwrought, but I dropped the bag obediently.

As she started up the staircase it occurred to me that I did not know her name. Frank, I knew, called her Signora Bandini, but even in my abysmal ignorance of the amenities between the classes I felt instinctively that this was a violation of the ethics involved.

"What am I to call you?" I asked, or I think that is what I asked. At least she understood and paused on the stairway. "I am called," she replied stentoriously, "Ber-r-r-nar-di-na." The r's rolled impressively up at least to the second landing.

"Ah...*grazie*," I murmured, knowing full well I could never negotiate that name, mine being the kind of tongue that doesn't trill.

As I followed her up the stairs my mind was busy with the major problem of breaking down "Ber-r-r-nar-di-na" into something I could handle—"Berna?" "Dina?" Her formidable broad back preceded me across the big salon and into the bedroom and I forgot the problem of nomenclature in my delight in the room.

The soft light of afternoon fell goldenly through the drawn curtains and illuminated the room in all its delicate details. French doors opened onto a tiny balcony, and both doors and windows were amply curtained with unglazed chintz, a rosebud pattern on white. On the wide, low bed was an enormous matching counterpane extending like a bridal veil out onto the parquet floor. On the mirror-topped dressing table beside the full-length mirror stood an exquisite blue glass lamp shaded in white lace, while below it two alabaster birds admired their reflections and seemed to symbolize the simple charm and taste of the room. (Simple? That school-of-Botticelli Madonna framed above the bed was a more accurate gauge of the place, but I hadn't read the inventory wherein it was listed at 350,000 lire.)

The woman set down the bags and opened the French doors and I looked out into the green coolness of a grove of ancient bay trees where, all the mornings after, birds sang to wake us (assuming we had ever got to sleep), their early morning tunings-up mingling with the thin, distant chiming of monastery bells and the singing of scores of little boys initiating the God-dominated activities of another busy day in the neighboring orphanage with ten or twelve well chosen hymns and chants.

"*Grazie*, Ber...Ber..." I began heroically as the maid prepared to leave me alone in my room. A look of compassion spread across her amorphous features. "I am also called Maria," she said helpfully, and added, making meaningful gestures toward my person and the valises, "The *Signora* will want to change into something more comfortable."

I was wearing slacks and I was perfectly comfortable, so I had to consider how I could improve my situation. Feeling, however, that something in the way of a change was expected of me, I thought of my long, cotton print housecoat—though I had never hitherto donned it at *this* hour of the day—and unlocked the bag which contained it. It was creased, of course, from long folding though quite presentable to my uncritical eye, but she assured me it needed ironing and she bore it off to the lower regions. I was ignorant, then, of the ceremonial pressing of anything that has been packed, and since I had been ironing my own clothes for more years than I care to mention, it gave me a pleasant, unwonted sense of being taken care of. *Dear* Maria. I would do something nice for her some day, I decided.

To pass the few moments the pressing would require, I sorted out my things and went to the bathroom to remove a considerable part of the Italian terrain from my person.

Maria, with her terrifying poise and her air of having everything so well in hand, had increased my sense of being a guest in a strange house, so when I entered the bathroom and saw my husband's grubby little kit in which he has carried his shaving items all over the world—spurning the numerous gifts of fitted leather cases pressed upon him by well-meaning relatives—I felt as if I had encountered a familiar face on a desert island.

I dallied over my bathing and went back to the bedroom, but there was no sign of the pressed garment. I moved from window to window and studied the views of the Roman countryside, the convent-studded hills, the blue peaks of mountains rimming the horizon even as in my native West. I examined minutely the great salon and planned out two or three ways it could be improved. I explored another bedroom which opened off it, and sat down finally in an enormous green velvet chair to wait. But still no sign of Maria.

I was considering ringing the bell, or just getting back into my slacks, but then I heard steps on the stairs. It had been nearly an hour and surely she would be full of apologies for the delay. Ah, but that was before I knew Italy where time is of no consequence. A few months later I would have appreciated that a new record in ironing speed had just been established.

Maria was as impressively composed as ever, and wanted to know if I would take tea here or downstairs. Downstairs, I decided hastily, and thank you I did *not* need any help getting into a thing I had been wearing every morning for too many years, even if it did give a pleasant illusion of elegance when it was freshly done up.

A few moments later, trailing my five yards of old muslin down the staircase, the Roman anodyne began to work and I began to feel helpless and cherished and ladylike and for about ten minutes I forgot that I was, in reality, a very capable and independent American woman and no nonsense. You don't get slightly bowed legs from lying on a chaise longue—not if you were brought up on a Montana ranch, you don't.

But I was mesmerized by the awesome assurance of Maria. With a *"faccio io"* this and a *"faccio io"* that, she took everything out of my hands. She summoned in the children, she served the tea, she put away the linens. She showed me around the house.

There was the entrance hall, first of all, now dominated by luggage. Beyond it was the "solarium," bleak and austere, furnished with green-painted wrought iron chairs and glass-topped tables. Standing against a panel of opaque glass was a huge, intricate and bird-less birdcage. Century plants in fluted jardinières on pedestals had been augmented, for my arrival, by bowls of oleander. Beyond the glass wall was the sound of cascading water which Maria explained as *"la fontana,"* a generic term for any running water which, however, left one free to imagine a decorative item complete with goldfish, and not merely the laundry tubs as it turned out to be.

Down a long red-carpeted hall flanked on either side by antique tables and chairs was the dining room, bathed in honeyed light that fell through a skylight over which branches had been placed to break the noontime sun. We saw ourselves approaching in an enormous gilt-framed mirror mounted above a gilded console table. Two seventeenth century statuettes of the "fop and merveilleuse" genre admired each other from opposite ends of the console with expressions quite as arch as if their hands had not been broken and the toes of their buckled pumps chipped. Maria touched them in an awed way and remarked that they were *"molto costosi,"* a verdict borne out by the inventory where they were listed at 100,000 lire despite their disfigurements.

I tested gingerly an L-shaped silken divan in one corner of the room and Maria seemed to be holding her breath. It was obviously not meant to be sat upon lest its damask fall apart. Among the various paintings, tiles, holy water fonts, and other items of varying antiquity which adorned the walls, I stopped to study two hideous little paintings on glass representing, as nearly as I could make out, either the delivery of the head of Saint John on a platter or some equally gory episode not exactly suited to a dining room.

Opening off the dining room with large glass doors was *"lo studio,"* large, square, simply furnished in light modern tones. A stage-size curtain of sea-green chintz drawn across the enormous panel of windows gave a sort of aquarium-like light to the place.

Arrived at down the red-carpeted hall in the opposite direction and through a room indicated as the "office"—a good long food-cooling distance from the dining room—was the enormous kitchen. It was adequately furnished, by Italian standards, with one old-fashioned kitchen cabinet, a two-burner gas plate, a tiny icebox with a broken latch, and a marble-topped table. The great black iron range was only a place to set things for it had been inactivated as a cooking appliance long since by soot-choked flues and caked grates. A thin stream of cold water flowed continuously from the single faucet over the granite sink. A long counter of marble ran the length of the kitchen under the wide windows which, if you pulled back the ancient curtains that covered them, gave out on the choicest vista of the entire house—poppy-studded fields, a countryside of villas and monasteries, and an expanse of blue mountains in the distance.

The kitchen floor had about a four percent grade so that the marble-topped table in the center had to have two legs shorter than the others. This sloping floor was a housekeeping convenience, as I was to learn, for you could simply upend a bucket of water at the high side and swish it down across the tiles and flush it out a drain into the fields.

Maria opened the credenza and pointed out to me, with evident pride in her own thoughtfulness, the space she had arranged for "my things." Since "my things" included an entire trunkful of kitchen equipment, the two shelves she had cleared of Bandini food and utensils seemed a trifle inadequate, but there seemed no way at the moment I could point this out without risking offense. Oh well, I would temporize by unveiling only a few at a time of the marvelous American gadgets I had brought along.

Only my checkered background kept me from being thoroughly dismayed by this enormous kitchen with its tiny islands of broken-down equipment, its few shelves, its obsolete range. My cooking, like my darkroom puttering, has been done in some pretty odd places during the course of a nomadic career, including a windowless closet over an oil burner. I had escaped burns and asphyxiation under harrowing circumstances and had come out with triumphant apple pies before this. I fully expected to do so again, just as soon as I got organized.

Getting organized proved to be an extended delaying action, however. My self-confidence had been initially shaken by the calm possessiveness of Maria, by the ubiquitous Bandini effects, and by the manner in which the custodian's family seemed to be entrenched in the lower regions of the house.

There was another hazard, however, which presented itself, and for which nothing in my previous experience had prepared me. In all my wandering I had never had to cope with a kitchen infested with *people*. Cockroaches, yes, silverfish, naturally, in certain places—but people!

It was not just the Bandinis themselves, though I had a horror of going into the kitchen and finding them grouped around the marble-topped table, napkins tucked under chins, elbows firmly placed on either side of large bowls of spaghetti—but the Bandinis had friends. Their friends were chiefly the members of the "good" peasant's household, the Garofanis—carnations in English. At whatever hour of the day I decided it was opportune for me to start whipping up some special family delicacy and went into the kitchen fully determined to do so, I would find a bright bouquet of Garofanis at the kitchen table. Rosy faced, white toothed, smiling, they sat on comfortably and said *"Buon giorno"* good naturedly, but they did not rise to make way for me and it was obvious that they belonged there, not I. Whereupon I would peer around momentarily as though I had just been on a routine inspection of the kitchen, say *"Buon giorno"* again and retire in considerable confusion, leaving them to their endless gossiping with Maria.

Thus my worthy intentions toward the kitchen duties were stymied. Well, I would try to help out in some other way, though to be perfectly honest I could not see that Maria was suffering from an overload of work. Her husband helped her with the heavy jobs, the carpet beating, the mopping and such. There was a beautiful, Junoesque young woman who came once a week to do the washing, including that of the Bandini family since Maria complained of rheumatic pains in her hands whenever she was obliged to put them in cold water. And every afternoon Maria found time for her siesta. She would send her child to me to say that should I require any services for the next two hours Rita would attend to them as *"la Mammina"* would be sleeping.

However, since Bandini had already suggested once or twice in an offhand and diffident manner that, the *Signora* having arrived, surely we would be taking on another maid, I felt I must bestir myself and relieve Maria of some of the duties to forestall having any more people under our roof and living at our expense.

Obviously the place to begin was with my own room. But Maria had prevented this by her habit of getting us safely settled at the breakfast table, then dashing up to do the room before we had finished. One morning, however, Maria was unaccountably detained in the kitchen and when we finished breakfast I discovered my bed still unmade. I proceeded to make the bed and to straighten the room a bit and then went down for a morning look at the garden.

I was standing at the little gate looking over at the parsley, and beyond at the neighboring fields where a pair of great white oxen with six-foot horn span were drawing a ridiculously small cart, when the lightning struck—and from behind.

"*Signora!*" I heard the booming voice of Maria and her steps crunching across the courtyard gravel. I turned to find her confronting me, the picture of outrage. "Why," she demanded in words so simple and elemental that I scarcely realized they were Italian, "*Why have you made your bed?*"

If a six-foot gendarme in a busby had suddenly confronted me and asked me why I had stolen the Vatican jewels I couldn't have been more startled—or more completely unaware of any crime committed. Nevertheless, in this case, I *was* guilty. I *had* made my bed. If this be treason, I thought—but there was nothing I could say. It was one thing to understand Maria, it was another thing to make myself understood. I wanted to say, "Why, I always make my own bed. Girl and woman for the past twenty-odd years I have been making my own bed mornings, so what?" But my Italian was too embryonic. I had to resort, in this crisis, to the classic Latin gesture which I had already learned, a shrug of the shoulders, an outward turning of the palms, and a smile with the corners of the mouth turned down meaning "Who knows?"—one of the best evasive answers ever devised.

Maria turned on her heel and went back into the house. I understood that I had violated some basic principle, but I was as yet too green to appreciate how completely I had fractured the amenities, too ignorant of the ancient and complicated stratification of old world society to know that the gravest offense to a servant is to be competent in his line of work, thereby robbing him of his one accepted point of superiority.

Maria continued to be polite thereafter, but she was a shade more aloof, and she was not so quick to snatch every minutest chore from my hands with a "*faccio io*—I'll do it."

Even yet we might have propped up the wobbly structure of my Signorial pedestal if it had not been for a tactical error on the part of the United States army. There was really nothing personal in A.M.G.

(Allied Military Government) deciding, the very week I arrived in Rome, to discontinue army rations to war correspondents' families. But to the Bandinis, who had been sharing our ration for many months, it was a grave blow. All that wonderful meat! Those whole livers they had had to pass on to their friends since they themselves did not care for liver. All those cans of fruit! The flour. The sugar!

The army's maneuver was certainly ill-timed for me. Maria must have suspected the new *Signora's* hand in the killing off of the golden goose. Certainly it was just the sort of thing you could expect from a lady who would make her own bed!

6

Sleep At Your Own Risk

Where I grew up, the house was never locked. Maybe you hooked the west screen door at night in case it blew open and the cats got in, but nobody could remember what had become of the key to the kitchen door. The front door had a night lock which was only a nuisance since we children sometimes played with it and accidentally shut out some member of the family who thereupon had to walk all the way around to the back to get in. Over the windows was nothing more impenetrable than a fly screen, or even cotton mosquito netting if the screen had rusted out. Summers the sashes would be up and a burglar could have entered as easily as a passing breeze, except we never thought of burglars.

I had not expected post-war Italy to be as safe as a western ranch or a Wisconsin village, or even suburban Chicago, but nothing had prepared me for the charged atmosphere that enveloped the House of the Four Winds.

Bandini promptly initiated me into the ritual of fear. It was still early evening of that first day when the house had seemed the epitome of peace. Frank had not yet come back from returning the truck and driver, when Bandini knocked at the salon door and with a polite "*permesso*" came in. "I must close the windows," he said, making a key-turning motion with his hand. I was a little dismayed at having the day so soon shut out, but I lacked the words to protest, and besides I had already begun to suspect that here the little details of housekeeping were not in my hands.

Bandini moved from window to window, pulled to the louvered shutters on the outside and secured them with iron hasps. Then he closed the panes of glass and, over these, solid wooden shutters. The hall, the bathroom, the salon, Marta's bedroom—one after the other all securely closed against the night while I listened to the unfamiliar sound of sliding bolts and closing latches.

When he came to my bedroom I made a feeble effort to protest. "*É necessario?*" I asked. "*Si, si, si, si!*" cried Bandini. He motioned me to the window and pointed outside. I saw that a great terrace lay just outside the window. From the far edge of the terrace a succession of tiled, gently sloping roofs covered the houses of the peasants who worked the neighboring fields.

"*Pericoloso,*" said Bandini, waving his hand toward these. "*Brutta gente.*"

Perilous I understood, and the other phrase must imply that our neighbors were unsavory characters. Among the Italian syllables I picked out one or two that conveyed some meaning. "*Rubato il motore,*" could only mean that we had been robbed of a motor, so I gathered that our man knew what he was about and I offered no further resistance to his operations.

When Frank came home I emerged rather shaken from my redoubt on the second floor and asked him if it was true about the motor. Yes, it was true. The motor which pumped water to the tanks in the attic had been installed, brand new, just before he moved into the house. It was in a little room off the dining room (you noticed that new door there by the tile stove?)—well, the next night the motor was stolen. The outside door had been broken open and the thing just disconnected and hauled away. When the new motor was installed— the second new one, that is—the outside door had been sealed off and an entrance to the furnace room cut through from the dining room, hence the new door.

I began to have some grudging respect for Bandini's bolting and barring, and qualms about my new home. Fear was a dimension I had not yet become accustomed to. I walked around the ground floor to find windows and doors secured with various devices of iron and wood. About this time, there was a tremendous noise like thunder which made me leap in terror, but Frank assured me it was only the iron door, the *saracinesca*, being rolled down over the front entrance.

"Is the drawbridge pulled up?" I asked with a feeble attempt at lightness.

All of these precautionary measures were directed impersonally toward all the wandering and predatory characters following in the wake of the war who, however needy and pitiful they might be, still had to be guarded against. In addition there was a conspicuous lack of faith in the inhabitants of the adjacent buildings who, judged on the basis of their personal habits and appearance, were indeed "*brutta gente.*" How many people lived under those adjoining roofs, or what relationship they bore to each other, nobody seemed to know. But of those we saw carrying on a rather feeble facsimile of farming in the fields, there was a cadaverous, grim old man, presumably the grandfather. There was a black-garbed old woman, ponderously shapeless. There were a couple of young and sinister looking men with lank black hair, their faces conspicuously and constantly adorned by American cigarettes in a day when cigarettes were currency. There were also various youngish women, children, dogs, cats, and goats.

Until our advent these people had evidently had the run of the place, passing in and out of our gate, cutting through the yard on their way to and from the neighborhood fountain, pointing out spots of interest, such as the swimming pool, to their frequent visitors with a proprietary air.

They had big trucks that came and went at odd hours of the night, and everybody supposed they were engaged in some sort of black market operations in wheat or sugar or some other scarce commodity, with possibly a little thievery thrown in. At all events they were dirty, unsmiling, and unkempt, and our hedges were their latrines. They were in marked contrast to the Garofanis, who were all strapping, hearty, rosy-cheeked and vivacious, and whose beautifully tended fields attested to their industry.

Some months of occupying the villa before our arrival had left their mark on my husband's generally sanguine disposition. I found him a nervous householder with a tendency to listen for strange sounds and to get up in the middle of a meal and look out to see what was going on in the foreground or the middle distance of our immediate landscape. I suppose it was only a natural reaction for one who had so recently gone through the ordeal of signing an Italian lease, and upon whose conscience hung heavily the precise value of every item of furniture and bric-a-brac, all mounting up to millions of lire.

It took some weeks and many accounts of neighborhood robberies (including the story of the Mother Prefect in a nearby school who awoke in the night to see a dark shape moving stealthily across the hallway toward the school's safe, and could not decide whether it was better to scream for help or merely to pray) before the concept of actual danger became fixed in my mind. And once fixed, a sense of security became dependent upon the nightly ritual of locking up, and upon the presence of other adults, preferably male, in the house. Not to mention the cold comfort of a gun within reach.

Life took on a new dimension, but it was not a widening or a broadening or a deepening of the planes, it was a dimension that narrowed and warped and distorted—the dimension of fear. Still, it made you aware of how darkness—night itself, for which you might long have had a sentimental attachment—became the enemy. The not seeing. The being surrounded by an impenetrable obscurity in which things moved and deeds were committed, terror receded or approached. It made you kin to the frontier grandma with the rifle across her lap, to the bivouacked soldier from Hannibal all the way down to Willie and Joe. Sleep at your own risk.

7

The Tongue of Dante

I have always had a gift for words. At seven I had a vocabulary which made me the pride of the teacher and the laughingstock of the second grade.

Through the succeeding years of what is euphemistically known as my education, I specialized in ululating, multi-syllable, esoteric words, never—unless cornered—condescending to the simple, one-syllable variety. I prided myself on originality of expression and coined words with a counterfeiter's abandon. Not that I was ever a great conversationalist. I suffer from a form of aphasia under duress which in some quarters might be considered stupidity but which I prefer to think of as an interesting aberration, an affliction which results in embarrassing pauses while I am groping for the bon mot.

In the relative tranquility of my own circle, however, I have always been able to construct limpid if not immortal sentences. In short, I felt I had the English language fairly well under control so that even strangers with whom I engaged in conversation could tell I had gone at least as far as the eighth grade.

One may imagine, then, that it came as something of a shock when my husband, after years of patient application to the grindstone, was duly rewarded by being assigned as a foreign correspondent to Rome, and I was faced with the painful alternatives of learning Italian or—heaven forbid—of being unable to express myself.

Forthwith I invested eagerly in a record course of the Italian language, but alas, the time was all too short. Frank had already gone to Europe, and Marta and I were to follow. There was an interval of about two months when I could apply myself to the record course and this, considering my native cleverness, should have been adequate, but unfortunately there were various other things to be done during those two months. Visualizing the great vacuum that allegedly existed in Italy in the way of food, clothing, household equipment, sanitation, and measures for personal safety, I was confronted with the necessity of assembling everything from powdered eggs to a private arsenal.

Between making out innumerable lists of innumerable things to be packed for the journey, buying and packing same, whipping together a wardrobe for myself and Marta, attending to endless details of family finance, belongings, and passports—between all these I listened with a somewhat distracted ear to the gravel voice of a certain Professor Orvizzi as conveyed to me on a cheap portable phonograph whose tendency to run down suddenly left the good professor apparently gasping his last.

I had gone through the first few records covering such useful items as an exchange of pleasantries regarding health and the weather with their usual superficial deviations, interspersed with appropriate expressions of caution, sympathy, and dismay. I had learned how to direct a taxicab and how to register at a hotel. But through no fault of Professor Orvizzi, as it turned out, none of this was to prove very useful to me in my early housekeeping adventures when what I needed to know were such phrases as "Do not put so much oil in the salad," "We are not accustomed to garlic," or "Why do you always skip the corners when you mop the floor?" Still, I had acquired a rudimentary knowledge of the language, which was to come in very handy even though when I tried to emulate the cadences of Professor Orvizzi people invariably asked me if I had *mal di gola*.

I staggered through the first months in Italy and gradually commanded a list of the common vegetables, household appliances, articles of clothing, and parts of the body. I was, in fact, doing quite well—I thought. I even began to have a dim knowledge of idioms so that I knew you don't "mop" a floor but "give it the cloth." Still, the subjects in which I was competent to construct three-word sentences were not likely to enchant a cultured Italian, whose knowledge of domestic problems might be limited to the pushing of a bell. I suffered acutely from inferiority complexes when Italian friends came to call. I could understand them pretty well, even to following a spirited political harangue, so long as I had an unobstructed view of their hands, but there was almost never a point at which I could get into the discussion myself by exclaiming dramatically, "Give it the cloth!" or even, "There's too much oil!", though the latter phrase is a not inappropriate interjection somewhere during the course of many Italian conversations.

Obviously it was a choice of learning more Italian or developing frustration neuroses from constantly bottling up the devilishly clever ideas that kept coming to my mind.

We had employed a "*signorina*" for Marta, a near-sighted spinster who preferred to carry on her lessons in the darkest corners indoors or under the gloomiest arbor out. I approached this *signorina* on the subject of an English-speaking Italian tutor who might come to give me lessons. What I had in mind was something informal and conversational and no being trapped into any involved consideration of the subjunctive mood. Somebody to teach me the Italian equivalent of phrases I had always found useful such as, "This seems to me an understatement," or "Your logic eludes me," or even, in extreme cases, "I couldn't agree with you more."

The *signorina* would see what she could find.

A few days later she reported that there was an Italian lady living at the house of the nuns who would be only too delighted to come to teach me Italian. I agreed to try her out. The next morning there arrived at our door a museum piece straight out of the pages of Dickens—battered black felt hat perched on crinkly yellowish hair; sharp features; musty black suit; pointed high laced shoes—the whole giving the impression of something that should be hung out to be aired.

"So you wish-ed to be instructed in Italian?" she asked acridly in antique English.

Yes, I agreed, that was the general idea. "I do know a little Italian," I said modestly, and tried to make it clear that I had thought both Marta and I might benefit from some casual instruction.

"Yes, yes, yes," she said briskly, "we shall see, we shall see."

I had certainly had no intention of jumping so precipitously into culture. I had intended testing it with a toe first, at least. But I had an uncomfortable feeling that I was about to be given a vigorous push off the deep end. My instructress was eager to begin. She seized Marta who had been hovering about, and set her firmly on her lap. Marta was never one to be fussed over and I saw her recoil at this intimate arrangement.

"Let us see what you can learn," cried the tutor, full of enthusiasm and the breath of garlic. She pointed to the floor. "*Pavimento!*" she cried. She pointed to the wall, "*parete!*" To the windows, "*finestre!*" The curtains, "*tende!*"

"*Pavimento, parete, finestre, tende,*" she repeated like a drill sergeant with a particularly stupid squadron. "*Pavimento, parete, finestre, tende!*"

Marta was speechless. She had been playing with the custodian's child for months now and she knew all these common words and a good many more, but to have them reeled off at her like this as if her life depended upon repeating them accurately was too much for her. She refused to open her mouth. I make no pretension to being a teacher, but my instinct told me this was scarcely the way to inspire a child to higher learning. For the moment, however, I was stymied by uncertainty as to whether this specter simply knew nothing about the art of pedagogy or was employing the accepted Italian method.

"Quickly now," cried the tutor, "repeat after me: *pavimento, parete, finestre, tende!*" Marta was rigid as a ramrod and her reddening face was a study in torment.

"*Signorina,*" I interrupted timidly, "I believe if we began by talking about things which are of interest to a child of this age—"

She glared at me. Clearly she thought me an interfering fool. However, she inadvertently relaxed her grip for a moment and Marta escaped like an eel and fled outdoors.

"Very well," said the *Signorina* grimly, "let us see what *you* know." I felt like a cornered rat and my well-known aphasia blanked out any Italian I may once have known. "Well, commence!" she ordered. "Speak to me in Italian."

The only thing I could think of was "Now is the time for all good men..." but since I was not warming up on a typewriter it seemed a little abstruse. "Quickly!" she cried as if she had five hundred other pupils waiting for her attention. "I must find out how much you know, or how can I begin teaching you?"

This was so patently reasonable a statement that I gulped and began. "I only speak kitchen Italian," I said in what I thought were recognizable words, but my tutor looked at me with a shocked expression.

"*What* are you trying to say?" she shrilled. I drew a deep breath and tried again, a little louder.

"But what *is* this you are trying to tell me?" She leaned into my face and her tone suggested that I, an underling, had garbled some important state message. It even crossed my mind that there might be some sinister double entendre to my innocently uttered phrases.

Meekly, in English—and I think even it was a bit broken—I explained. "I was trying to say that I only speak what I call 'kitchen Italian.'" She was not only not amused by my feeble pleasantry, she had an injured air as though I had misled and deluded her.

"But *this* is not Italian at all," she snorted. "Who wishes to speak only to the servants? Italian is the language of the immortals. It is the most beautiful of languages. It is the tongue of Dante! It must be learned from the *beginning!* Now say to me, 'I am an American.'"

"*Io sono Americano,*" I said desperately, crippled genders falling all about me. Her groan was eloquent. I knew without being told that I had just pulled the tongue of Dante out by the root.

"But you *said* you knew Italian," she said witheringly. "You know nothing *what-so-ever.* Now I see that we must begin from the *beginning!*"

The hell we will, I said under my breath in pig Latin. Maybe I knew nothing *what-so-ever* of classical Italian—I really hadn't claimed to, had I?—but I had been getting along for three months after a fashion and I already spent forty-some or was it sixty-some dollars for the canned services of Professor Ignazzi or Orvizzi or whoever he was, and I certainly was not going to begin repeating, "*Buon giorno, Signora,* how-are-you-today-I-hope-you-enjoy-good-health" or even, "Will-you-take-the-train-or-the-steamship-to-Genoa?"

"You are quite right, *Signorina,*" I said with elaborate politeness through my teeth. "As you see, I know nothing about Italian. We will begin at the beginning." (We will go back to the point at which I never heard of you, I thought.) "But I prefer to start the lessons tomorrow as I have another engagement today."

"Very well," she croaked. "Good day, missus. I will return tomorrow." With which evil threat she left me. And Marta, who had observed (from the crotch of the mulberry tree which she had never previously been able to reach without a boost) the departure of this apparition across the courtyard, flew into the house and we collapsed upon each other.

"Oh, Mommie! Do I have to have *her?*" Marta asked.

"No," I said, "she won't *do!* Tonight you must run over to your lesson *signorina* and tell her to tell this *signorina* at the *suore* that we have changed our minds. Tell her we're going back to America. Tell her *anything,* but make her understand we don't want that woman tomorrow!"

Thus came to an abrupt end my formal indoctrination in the intricacies of the language of the immortals. I hate to say it, but at that moment I was pretty sure the tongue of Dante had me licked.

8

An Island in Time

Young children and old country places belong together. They have a natural affinity.

Children who grow up in streamlined modern homes and efficiency apartments probably find something to compensate them in part for the absence of cellar-ways, lofts, vine-hung garden walls, and secret nooks, but surely their storehouse of memories is less rich than ours who, on grown-up sleepless nights, can return to a beloved attic to stir, in memory, its golden dust, start its mice from their long-vanished nests, shake out the folds of antique costumes, admire the painted flowers on long-unwarmed chamberpots...

To hear again the flowing of poplar leaves across the roof, the rustle and twitter of swallows in the eaves... sun shafting through a chink in the gloom of the tower-room, laying a harness of light on an abandoned hobby-horse... the stillness and the peace that suggest, somehow, spectacles put aside, gnarled hands folded, the closed book marked at a favorite passage... "Oh world invisible, we view thee..."

Or of cellars... the smell of apples, the gleam of rows of canned fruits and vegetables blending their muted, summery colors on cobwebby shelves... the mounds of potatoes with their long pale sprouts... of onions describing gracefully in the darkness Hogarth's celebrated line.

Or of barns and outbuildings...

It was strange that during those first few summer months at the villa, in the exquisite bell-clear mornings, as I sunned myself on the warm red tiles of the upper terrace, my mind kept going back to a haunt of my own childhood, an ocean and a continent away, back to the "honey house" on a ranch in Montana, or more specifically, to the top of the honey house.

The honey house itself was forbidden territory. We might damage the alabaster combs of honey stored there. We might leave the door ajar and the bees, prying eternally at the crevices, might get in to retrieve their precious store. But the top of the honey house was our territory. A partitioned cubicle of a room at one end of the larger area of the ice house (where winter-harvested ice was stored under sawdust), the honey house was ceiled off below the gable of the ice house and rose like a square island in the sea of sawdust.

When the ice harvest was fresh in winter, the top of the honey house was easily accessible but then, with the cold that set the beams to creaking and left all the nail-heads white to frost, it interested nobody. As the season advanced into summer and the ice melted or was consumed, the roof of the honey house was ever more difficult to reach and hence a more desirable objective. Our favorite cat had her kittens there. Sparrows ticked across the shingles close over our heads. The fine, flowery smell of honey mingled with the smell of sawdust and of weathered, sun-toasted wood of roof and sidings.

It was a marvelous hideaway with all the attributes of remoteness and secrecy, the delicious peril attendant upon scrambling up and getting down, or straying too near the edges and falling off into the sawdust below. Nobody knew where we were and nobody cared, for it was summer and we were young. It was an island in time, a treasure island, and it even had its own hoard of plunder which we dipped into without a qualm of conscience, namely the sweet dried prunes which generations of chipmunks had carried laboriously from the orchard and stored in the sawdust-filled walls in the mistaken notion that they would be safe.

How good they tasted, those stolen and undoubtedly germ-laden sweets, and how the special flavor of them came back to me there on a Roman terrace, and the smell of the honey house, and behind my closed eyelids, the amber, sun-flecked peace of that raftered retreat, the special flavor of a time and state of being.

Always since leaving the villa, in my casual reflections about that ancient, disintegrating, but withal charming place, when I think of those sunny hours on the terrace I experience a telescoping of memories so that what I hear in my mind is not the scurrying of lizards across red tiles or the rattle of ox-carts in the road below, but rather the chirping of sparrows, the drone of bees, the singing of hens basking on the sunny side of the honey house.

For a long time it puzzled me, this inevitable association, but finally it became clear. The villa with its niches and its crannies and its remoteness from the clamor of the world, had that special flavor. I was no longer a child, but there for the first time in years I could be lazy with a clear conscience, with no nagging awareness of unfinished chores, meals to be got, babies to be changed. Not since my honey house days had I had such a windfall of time, such a treasure of carefree idleness which is the essence of childhood. It was some honey-like fragrance of flowers growing round about, plus the toasted-wood smell of the ancient shutters that recreated, out of all the diverse scenes of my childhood, the beloved honey house.

But there was something else, some further spice in the air that flowed over this new island in time. It was the then incompletely realized fact that here, for our city-bred, apartment reared child, was a golden treasury of experiences, of sensations, of sights and sounds and smells which would spin themselves one day into a spider-fleece of memories ever after to festoon her life. Here in a foreign land she had not wanted to come to, she would harvest figs from the thistles of the loneliness, the inconveniences we might have to submit to in living where time stood still and our lives had been turned backward a generation from the too-tidy, too-bland living of her mid-twentieth-century American heritage.

From my terrace I would hear her voice from time to time, and the voice of Rita, and of Paula and Teresa, the *contadini* children. I would hear their running steps on the gravel of the courtyard. They would be on the knoll where the bay trees, with great gray trunks and bark like elephant hide, provided a shadowy retreat out of the sun. They would be running races up and down the *viale*. They would be under the long arbor that ran the length of the swimming pool, dark and secluded as a room with its heavy mat of vines. Or they might be down in the pool itself, wading in the water that was only three or four inches deep now that a control had been put on the flow so that the pool no longer could be filled.

This pool, one of the most persuasive talking points when the leasing of the house was under consideration, had been brimming with water and overflowing into the surrounding fields. Large carp and many smaller fish testified to the fact that through wars and water-famine the pool had still remained filled. It was exceptionally large, probably a hundred feet in length with a depth of four or five feet. In the center was a structure of masonry with a double arch topped by a statue of a child and a swan.

Shortly after we took the house, however, the authorities came and gaped in wonder at the flowing water and the filled pool. "This," they cried, "is a contravention." They clamped a control device onto the pipes so that the water to the pool was reduced to a trickle. The level receded and one morning the fish were found gasping their last on the nearly exposed floor of the pool.

Marta and I had never seen the pool in its glory. By the time we arrived in Italy the water was ankle deep except in the two dangerous deep sinkholes in the center on either side of the island. The island itself stood up on its concrete foundation, a grotesquerie without purpose now that the water no longer flowed under its arches and irises no longer grew from its niches. Even as a place for wading, however, the pool soon lost its appeal. Algae slimed the surface of the stagnant water. Frogs strung their eggs in hopscotch designs, water skippers skated across it. Tadpoles hatched and absorbed their tails, put forth legs and hopped away to the surrounding fields as delicate little green frogs.

As a place to observe nature, however, the pool had an appeal both fascinating and repulsive. Strange sorts of insects stalked about its margins. Scarabs rolled their balls of dirt in apparently aimless directions, falling on their armored heads when the ball chanced to roll too fast downhill, then scrambling anxiously back to it with their scalloped forefeet waving, ready to grasp their prize when they located it.

There were praying mantises whose reverent pose belied an alert and feral nature. There was a "crying beetle," a name we gave it after we heard the infinitesimal sobbing which originated in a bellows-like thorax. The better to observe the strange, elongated beetle, I had set a water glass over it, and in doing so had inadvertently caught one of its long legs under the edge of the glass. In protest the beetle set up its minute clamor which ceased when its leg was freed. There was the mole cricket which landed at our feet in the gravel seemingly from nowhere and was so outlandish a creature that we could not decide whether it was reptile or insect. Its strange, elongated, highly mobile head looked like that of a lizard. Its forefeet were mole-like, powerfully developed for digging. But from the thorax back it was insect. It tried frantically to burrow into the gravel and from the rear parts exposed you would have said it was a locust. When its reptilian head emerged, you were baffled to the point of assuming it to be some badly assembled and probably deadly creature from another planet. We saw only one as they are shy of the light and live underground.

And there were always the lizards, green and bright-eyed with jewel-like delicacy and precision, sunning themselves on the ledges and slipping away like shadows at one's approach.

Surrounding the pool were shrubs and roses and clumps of pampas grass. The cats slept under the bushes and the children shared their hideaways.

But even more fascinating than the pool with its multitudinous inhabitants, at least as a subject for fantastic speculation, was the cave, or what we thought of as the cave until we discovered that it was, in reality, an underground passageway with various branches, the extent of which we never fully explored.

The mouth of the cave was a brick archway without a door but with the remains of great hand-forged hinges, at one end of the mount where the bay trees grew. Ivy overhung it, and the steps leading downward into the dark, cavernous interior were littered with dead leaves and rubble. At the foot of the stairs the tunnel turned abruptly at right angles and led off under the courtyard in the direction of the swimming pool, and we assumed it ended there. The entranceway and the beginning of the tunnel we had explored with flashlight and apprehension, but when we came to a wall with only a small hole giving access to that part of the tunnel lying beyond, we did not explore further. Unquestionably there were skeletons and buried treasure beyond the wall, but the dankness and the bats and the cobwebs repelled us.

One morning some men representing the tram company came to our door and informed us that the trams were sinking into our tunnel. We looked at each other incredulously. Had the trams, then, taken to crossing our courtyard quite unbeknown to us? But no, the trams ran in the street as usual, a hundred yards beyond our house, and the earth was indeed giving way under their tracks in a line projected from the end of the known tunnel. "Our" tunnel, then, was an extensive affair and reached, probably, to the villa across the street which may at one time have been part of the same estate. As a matter of fact I suspected that our house was originally the barn. At all events, the tram company reinforced or filled in the abandoned tunnel under their rails, and we were inspired to further exploration on the near end.

Marta and Bandini undertook the expedition. He boosted her through the hole and scrambled after her with the flashlight. They found that the tunnel branched beyond the wall and that one passageway, lined with great spikes and hooks, led to the kitchen end of the house, though a door and stairway leading to it from the kitchens must long since have been sealed off and hidden under later additions. They found no treasure, but in the end nearest the house was indeed a skeleton—the remains of a cat—and the mystery of the stench which had permeated that part of the villa for a few weeks the previous year was finally solved.

And the villa had its attic. A third story sat like the top layer of a wedding cake above the wider roof of the second story. This floor was reached by a crude inside stairway. One entered a dusty chamber under the angle of the roof. The odor of chickens and rats was strong in the airless place and the floor was strewn with straw. Chickens were kept in highly unlikely places in Italian houses during the war and just after, on terraces and balconies, for example, so the fact of chickens in the attic may not have borne out my theory of this having once been the barn. At any rate the chickens were gone now and only the rats inhabited the upper regions.

Beyond this dusty room was a square room with whitewashed walls, one high window, and a peaked roof. It would have made a fine studio and perhaps had been in its prime a writer's or painter's retreat, but now it was the repository of odds and ends of furniture and bric-a-brac. The water tanks were at one side of the room and near them dangled bunches of tiny tomatoes for winter use. There were ancient fishnets, a spinning wheel, and various relics of the past. There were some locked trunks of the *padrone* of the villa, and to this room we had carried the bell jars of artificial flowers and other objects around the house which we did not care for in the decorative scheme, or which were too fragile to be left where they might be broken.

The children were not allowed to play in the attic, for it was the traditional room retained by the owners for storing some of their things and for giving an excuse to return to the house from time to time to check up on the tenants. When properly accompanied by an adult, however, the children went now and then to the attic to gaze at the relics with that particular speculative yearning we all feel toward things unused and abandoned.

Sometimes lying on the terrace, eyes closed against the brilliant sun, I concentrated on the sounds of the place. There were the convent and monastery bells which seemed to carry on a conversation. Perhaps they spoke only to their own order, but in their various tones and timings one could imagine greetings and responses, a bit of coded gossip, a complaint, a word of encouragement across the terraced hills.

From the fields rose the sharp "Aii!" of a peasant urging on his dove-grey oxen whose glacial pace was influenced neither by shouted command nor snapping whip. Great-wheeled carts rumbled and rattled along the cobbled streets. Sometimes a mule or donkey rasped out his creaky lament. From the bay trees and the mulberries of the courtyard came the day-long warble of small, shy birds.

But the sound that began and closed the day and marked it at frequent intervals from dawn to dusk was the singing of the children in the orphanage across the road. This concerted and disciplined singing, though it had a lusty note of real enjoyment, was still not the spontaneous, free outpouring we heard sometimes from the streets at night or from the fields by day, and it brought inevitably a certain overtone of poignancy.

My knowledge of the orphans was purely auditory, for I had scarcely glimpsed the hundreds of little boys whose lives were circumscribed by the walls surrounding the big, bleak building. But Marta, with the normal prerogative of childhood for peering through knotholes and cracks, reported that they were a drab bunch of little boys in very big shoes and very short pants, and that they all had shaved heads and wore little white cotton hats pulled down to their ears. They all, she insisted, looked exactly alike.

One morning as I lay daydreaming with the scents and sounds of summer all around me, and the little overalled barefoot moppet of my childhood self padding through my mind on well-remembered paths—suddenly the tempo of the singing from the orphanage changed and I forgot my reveries to listen. There was a special verve and zest to the song they were singing and I knew I had heard it before. Suddenly I realized they were singing an Italian version of "Aren't You Glad You're You?"

I thought of all the little shaved heads and the white cotton hats and the children who all looked alike to Marta, and thought how indomitably the yearning toward individuality yet surged up in each. I hoped the words carried the same meaning in Italian, that each little shave-topped orphan, though his very name may have been lost in the wartime shuffle, was really glad to be himself and to assert it so zestfully in the morning air. I felt reassured regarding orphanage life as I listened to verse after verse of the splendid rhythm. I was sure that Mr. Bing Crosby would be pleased to know that so lively a tune, thanks to his cinematic association with the Cloth, had found its way into what I took to be the rather dreary routine of the children in a Roman orphanage.

Memory makes a wide detour of winters in the villa. The very bones retain a sense of the chill that pervaded the big house. But there was the fireplace in the big salon and when it was lighted, smoking a little so that the afternoon sunlight from the south windows fell through a drifting blue veil, we drew the chairs close around the hearth warming our hands on the teacups and our feet by the flames.

No smoke is sweeter than the smoke of bay boughs. We had gathered the pruned branches of the bay trees and stored them with their leaves to dry for our winter fires, and thanks to an imperfectly functioning fireplace the house had a special winter fragrance.

Or there was the smell of roasting peppers. When the big green *peperoni* took on their autumn colors of crimson and yellow, they were roasted over gas flame in the kitchen until the skin was burned black so that it could be slipped off and the peppers cut up in strips to be eaten with salt, a little garlic, and olive oil.

The sharp, and at first unpleasant smell of roasting coffee beans was another characteristic scent in the villa. Green coffee beans were put into a little roaster and stirred over the heat until they were black and shining with oil.

If I remember, from another time and place, the song of meadowlarks along the lane, the restless drone of bees, the fine spicy aroma that pervaded a Montana ranch house at canning and pickling time, Marta from her Italian childhood will have other scents and other sounds.

When she is grown, when she is far removed in time and circumstance from those days, when responsibilities press in on her and the world seems not to have the glisten it once had, and nights sometimes yawn cavernous without sleep—to what sanctuary of the past will her memory return?

Will that be her "honey house," the decaying villa hiding its rotted woodwork under a veil of jasmine flowers? Will it be the smell of roasting peppers and toasting coffee that transports her from schoolroom or office to the great kitchen she once knew with its marble counters and its vine-framed windows that looked out to the Alban hills? Will she remember, at some busy intersection of her life, the singing of orphans from across the road, the chiming of bells from half a dozen hilltops above the city that is called eternal?

9

Patience, It Passes...

At a certain moment in early summer, the little red spider mites appear. British soldiers, we American children used to call them, thus innocently perpetuating historical prejudices. But the little redcoats, which we regarded erroneously as poisonous, were not so numerous in my part of the world. In Italy they appear as if by spontaneous generation and they are everywhere on the march at once, hurrying madly to some momentous appointment, attacking ferociously any of their fellows who impede their progress. A heavy rain will wipe them out for a few hours, but millions more quickly replace them and for a week or so every ledge and rock and clod is a-crawl with the minute crimson specks.

The first time I encountered them in Italy they were on the mashed potatoes, and I thought they were paprika, a seasoning which, so far as I knew, we did not then have on our pantry shelves. Maria must have found some in the market, I thought, pleased. But when the potatoes were passed to me, I discovered that it was not paprika, but a garnish of little red insects. But where did they come from? Even as I weighed the mystery, several more appeared on the tablecloth. Looking up, I realized that they must be tumbling down from the skylight which was directly above the table.

"Remove the *animali* from the potatoes," I said to Maria, "and tell Bandini to see what he can do to keep them from coming through the skylight."

"*Pazienza, Signora,*" Maria said. "Nothing can be done to prevent them coming through the skylight, like rainwater in its season, but the season passes. In a week there will be no more red *animali*. Meanwhile we can move the table to one side."

Like the rainwater? Does the rain also come through the skylight? Ah, yes, *Signora*. It comes through the skylight—and many other places as well.

How right she was we discovered when the rains began in November. I emerged from the bedroom into the upstairs salon one morning to find a steady little stream descending into the middle of the divan which I had moved to one end of the room from its accustomed place in the center. I rang the bell for Maria, but she appeared almost simultaneously, bucket in hand. She had anticipated the leak. "There will be a stream at the south end by the windows, also," she said complacently. "Be calm, I will wipe up the floor at once."

The south end stream was centered over an antique table which I had moved from the center of the room. The divan and the table were now shoved back toward the center. Had that arrangement, I wondered, been less a matter of taste than a meek acquiescence to the facts of life?

"How long has this been going on?" I asked Maria.

"I am here in this house two years," she answered, "and we have had these same leaks each season. I have put pans under that in the studio and I have moved the dining table from under the skylight."

Well, fortunately, the stone floors can't be damaged, I thought, but I suddenly realized that as Maria wiped up the water from the red tiles of the salon floor her cloth was turning red. The tiles were fading. I pointed this out to Maria. "Yes," she said, "we will have to repaint the tiles after the rains."

"Too bad," I said, "we have just waxed and polished them."

"*Si, Signora*, it is one of the problems."

But, *pazienza*, it was only in the heaviest rains that the bucket brigade was called out. In the gentler showers the roof was adequate, or so it seemed. But on the wall of the studio a damp spot kept spreading and spreading as the season went on. Presently it began to mildew so that a third of the wall was hideously mottled as if with a creeping, fatal malady. But by that time the studio had become too cold to be used, and it was closed off.

Little by little our living space contracted from the cold and we were finally confined to the dining room where there was a big tile stove. In the kitchen the Bandinis huddled around the old range which with much cajoling and persuasion produced a faint warmth if you sat very near it and could stand the smoke. We emerged from our warmed areas reluctantly and made hasty forays into the unheated parts of the house when some urgent necessity drove us to it. On state occasions we lighted the fireplace in the salon but it consumed tons of wood without appreciably lessening the chill five feet away from the hearth.

Lina, the housekeeper, who had been with us for a while that winter, suffered most acutely for she had to do the bedrooms and the unheated salon. She wore gloves when she made the beds and still got chilblains on her hands. Only Marta—fragile, weed-thin, ankles and wrists sprouting out of her garments—went around serenely in the cold house and didn't feel the cold at all.

But *pazienza*, spring would come.

10

This Woman! This House!

It probably is a result of having been born under the sign of Aries, but it never occurred to me until quite recently to doubt that there is nothing you can't have if you are persistent enough. As, for instance, my wanting a horse when I was little. It took years of patient badgering, but I eventually got a horse.

When I decided to take up photography as a hobby it never occurred to me that there might be circumstances under which it would be impossible to operate. It was a foregone conclusion that I would pack up my photographic supplies and take them along if I had to move my habitation from Minnesota to Italy. If there was electric current in Italy I could bring along everything else I might need. Anyone slightly brighter and less stubborn would have known that by the law of diminishing returns there might have been circumstances under which the product was scarcely worth the effort expended, but I was not yet receptive to reasonable ideas when I decided to pack my darkroom equipment into a trunk and take it along.

As a matter of fact, my husband aided and abetted this folly by writing, "There are plenty of places in this villa where we could set up a darkroom." From then on it was only a matter of several sprained fingers, frayed nerves, strained family relationships, and days of unremitting toil before the big enlarger was dismantled and packed into a trunk, together with all the hundreds of other items, mostly breakable, which an amateur photographer considers necessary to successful darkroom puttering. I would get my darkroom to Italy or die in the attempt.

When I saw the trunks coming out of the hold of the *Marine Carp* in a net that day in Naples and being dumped with a sickening klunk in a heap on the pier, I had many a misgiving about the wisdom of my decision, but when we opened the trunk later we discovered that the only thing to have suffered damage was the trunk itself, whose trays had given way under the load of heavy equipment they contained. So far, so good.

On my first inspection of the villa when Bandini showed me around from room to room, I had one eye cocked for a likely spot to establish a darkroom. Nothing seemed very promising, however. There was plenty of space and many an unused room, but none of them seemed to lend itself to my purpose.

The one part of the house Bandini had not shown me, however, was the storeroom. This was a locked room off the entrance hall and it had a glass door through which I could peer and get a vague impression of a room crowded with everything from extra jeep tires to boxes of army groceries and surplus furniture. What I could not see through the door, and what was revealed to me later when Frank came home and unlocked the room, was that beyond this room was another—a windowless, square cubicle about ten by ten feet, and it had a little marble basin with a water spout above it. Presumably this had been a sort of antique "powder room" and the other, opening off the *ingresso*, had been a place for guests to hang their wraps. In the inventory it was designated as the wardrobe room.

This inner cell, too, was full of miscellaneous stuff—trunks, boxes, supplies. But it had possibilities. The helter-skelter disarray could be systematized into something neat and orderly with canned goods stored on shelves made from the empty ammunition boxes salvaged from army castoffs, and the room would be ideal for a darkroom, even if the ornate little marble fountain did not produce water through its rusted pipes. The essentials were there—a large, square table, electric current, and only one small door to be covered to make it light-tight.

In a beaverish burst of activity I accomplished the rearrangement of the *cantina* almost single-handed. Because of some missing—or miscounted—rations in the early days of Frank's occupancy of the house, the help was not permitted access to this storeroom, and whenever spaghetti or sugar was required I had to issue it personally, a chore I found somewhat embarrassing until I came to realize that the locked *dispensa* was a natural condition of Italian life and implied no personal distrust of the current servant, but on the contrary marked the *padrona* as being sensible and prudent.

As one who had done darkroom puttering under strange and diverse conditions—once a tiny, waterless, airless bedroom closet under the slope of a roof, another time in a cramped little bathroom where the enlarger table straddled the toilet to the inconvenience of the family in general—this Roman darkroom seemed ideal. It was cool and spacious and light-tight.

But there was the matter of the current. In 1946 Rome was a city of flickering lights. When the lights were not actually off they were engaging in an exasperating game of blinking—off and on, off and on—or the power would diminish until the wires in the electric bulbs glowed in faint loops, and you watched them in a state of suspense not knowing whether the current would vanish entirely or be suddenly reanimated. Usually this painful process resulted in total darkness. Every dinner conversation in those days was punctuated by "Oh, oh! The lights!" Whereupon candles would be brought.

The lapses of current lasted from moments to hours. Sometimes you had the feeling, particularly during the blinking process, that someone was deliberately playing with the current, toying around with the public switch just to make everybody in Rome sit breathless waiting for the lights to come on or go off at his whim. But of course it was the disrepair of the lines, the lack of power all over the war-torn countries, and everyone suffered equally except possibly those who were totally without electricity in their houses or caves and so never missed it.

But it was not only the malfunctioning of the lighting system in general which plagued us at the House of the Four Winds. This antique pile of stone and stucco had problems unique unto itself. Having been added to and taken from over the course of the years at the whim of its current owner, its wiring was a patchwork affair. The entrance hall and the central core of the house were obviously the most antique and their wiring probably had been done about the time electricity first came into general use in the rural areas around Rome. As a wing was added here, a kitchen there, other circuits were added. When lights failed in the kitchen, they might still be burning in some other parts of the house, but half of the upper floor might be simultaneously without lights. The fuse which controlled this particular part of the house had to be searched out among the rafters and angles where the wires crept in and out of the wall, over doorways and around baseboards.

To cope with the complicated web-work of wires, we began calling in an electrician, a certain Signor Ferri, who was employed by the tram system at a maintenance station nearby. Ferri would grope among the beams and feel his way along baseboards until he came to the fuse, and presently we would have lights again. A few days later the lights would be out in the studio and dining room, or the bedrooms would be in darkness. Ferri would be summoned again and begin the groping and searching for another fuse at some other unlikely spot.

Between Ferri and me there developed a sort of pleasant antipathy. He was a repulsive looking man with yellowish white hair, a froglike face, and several missing front teeth among the misshapen, stained snags which still graced his smile. He was a man full of fine contempt for things in general—the Church, the Pope, the government, the British, the Italians, the aristocracy. I suspect at heart he was a Communist (as are so many thousands of other Italians like him for whom a lifetime of unremitting toil has brought neither happiness nor security nor the price of a decent funeral), for his one level of sympathy was the laboring man, although Ferri himself cultivated one long little-finger nail which is the Italian symbol for the white-collar worker, or at least for the worker whose job involves a little brainwork and special skill instead of being entirely of the hands and the back. It is a symbol affected chiefly by tram conductors, small office employees, and others of similar status.

Due, probably, to a combination of Ferri's Roman accent, his missing front teeth, and his original conviction that I did not understand any Italian and should be addressed only in infinitives or in isolated words, I was from the first unable to mesh mentally with the good Signor Ferri. He would, for example, point to some piece of equipment in his bag which resembled a hammer, and he would say to me with an upward inflection, *"Martello?"* (hammer) From this I was supposed to deduce not that he called the hammer-like object a hammer, but that he wanted me to bring him a hammer from our own supplies. When I looked blank and stupid he would simply point again and say, more loudly, "Hammer?" Since I had not mastered the Italian equivalent of "So what?" I could only look more and more confused while he lost his temper and sought out the maid muttering, *"Questa donna!"* (This woman!) as he disappeared from my presence. He did not even dignify me by saying *"Questa Signora!"* (This lady!) I knew I should have been insulted, but on the other hand there was Ferri's well-known contempt for the *Signori*, and his calling me *"Questa donna"* was probably in reality a sort of compliment.

In any event, *questa donna* would have understood more readily had he put his questions into a sentence—"Will you bring me a hammer?" or, "I lack a real hammer, will you bring me a proper one?"

Despite our mutual contempt, however, the visits of Ferri were often looked forward to with great eagerness and we welcomed him and his "briefcase" full of odd tools, bits of wire, parts of switches, pokes of plaster of Paris, with an elaborate hand-shaking courtesy. His electrical prowess was probably not great, but he was a handyman as well who could fix a toilet, lay a tile, put a hole through a wall for extending a gas connection just as readily as he could hunt up a faulty fuse, and we came to depend upon him in many a crisis.

"Call Ferri" became a household phrase. Often, however, the complicated wiring had even Ferri confounded. He would grope around the walls groaning over *"Questa casa!"* just as he groaned over my stupidity. When he couldn't lay his hand on the trouble within a reasonable time he would pack up his briefcase, put on his coat and, tapping his forehead, would say, *"Bisogno studiare un po."* (I must study a little on this.) He would depart to return another day after supposedly doing some intense mental work on the problem in question.

There was one quirk in the wiring of the house which all Ferri's "studying" never solved. In an angle of the outer wall where it adjoined the wall of the house, high up near the edge of the tile roof, was a little niche in which stood a figure of the Madonna and before it glowed a tiny orange light. The lacy branches of the jasmine had grown across it, but still the little light shone through, burning night and day.

The box in which were the various switches controlling the house lights was on the outside wall near this niche. Whenever Ferri had occasion to search for a blown fuse or do some wire patching, he had to come here to throw the switch. Nothing he ever did had any bearing on this perpetually burning light. Regardless of which circuit was interrupted, the light in the niche burned on. This was a matter which caused Ferri considerable brow tapping. *"Mannaggia!"* he would mutter, using a common Roman cuss word, "From where comes that light?" Certainly some day, he reasoned, he would turn up the circuit to which the vigil light was connected and solve the mystery of the light that never failed.

Obviously with the current so erratic and our own sick fuses constantly under the care of a specialist, all thought of darkroom work was out of the question for the time being. There came an interval, however, of relative stability. For some weeks the lights had functioned with unusual brightness and no failures of current. The fuses had held up under the strain of our electric iron, the pump, and the sewing machine. Finally, I thought, the time has come to try out the darkroom.

I got everything ready, cheerfully mixing chemicals in the kitchen while Maria took her afternoon nap and I had the place to myself. As a final check I went about the house turning on lights to see that all the various circuits were correctly functioning. Then I betook myself and my solutions to the darkroom. Fumbling at the door for the switch I confidently turned it. No light. I tried all the connections and extensions. No light. Well then, it must be another general shut-off that had occurred just at the moment I entered the room. Going out into the rest of the house I tried the lights there a second time. Everywhere in the whole house the lights functioned except in the darkroom!

"*Questa casa!*" I cried in a Snake Pit falsetto. "*Questa casa!*" It was only by the exertion of superhuman self-control that I refrained from drinking down the bottle of hypo.

Hysteria would get no pictures printed, however, so there was only one thing—the usual thing—to do. I went to the kitchen where the still dreaming Maria emerged sleepily from her quarters. "Call Ferri," I said.

When Ferri arrived, briefcase in hand, I led him grimly to my darkroom. "*Niente luce,*" I said, and he started toward the fuse that controlled the kitchen end of the house. "But no," I said, not without a certain satisfaction. "In the kitchen there is light. In the studio there is light. In the *salone* upstairs there is light"—mentioning each of the crucial sections of the already ascertained three circuits. "Only here in this room there is no light!"

Ferri looked momentarily baffled. Then his face glowed with a wonderful idea. At last he had it. At last he had found the other circuit. "*La Madonnina,*" he cried, rushing outdoors—"the little Madonna!"

Outside, behind the delicate screen of the jasmine leaves, the tiny light of the Madonna still burned faithfully in the niche. Ferri had a stricken look. "*Questa casa!*" he groaned. "*Dio mio, questa casa!*" He tapped his forehead and said he would have to think this one out and departed, his briefcase flapping violently against his legs.

But I was a beaten woman. If fate could single out this day, this hour, and the specific circuit I happened to be plugged in on to frustrate my efforts, then photography was obviously not for me. I can take a hint.

11

"La Signora É Delicata…"

The longest time my husband was ever absent—not excluding those five years during the war—was the six-week period of the Mediterranean cruise. That was an interval to which none of the normal measurements apply. Time was a millstone around the neck. It was a pain in the stomach. It was a crippled tortoise creeping backward toward a goal it had no desire to reach.

If I have spoken earlier only of the events of the day of his return, it is because I have had to steel myself to reconstruct the ordeal of those weeks during which I aged perceptibly from hour to hour and acquired a permanent sense of martyrdom, particularly when people ask us whether we travelled much during our years in Italy. This little pig, as it happened, stayed home.

Trips are always sought-for plums among the news staff, especially if they involve some sort of extended junket that promises to require a minimum of effort—something which happens only at blue-lunar intervals in a life devoted to following political campaigns and other natural disasters. Travelling assignments are usually handed out in rotation but for a prize such as this—six weeks at sea during the tender days of a Mediterranean spring—there was bound to be a certain amount of jockeying. While it was actually Frank's turn, we indulged in the possibly groundless suspicion that it had been offered him with the foregone conclusion that he would refuse, whereupon it would go to the next in line, the current fair-haired boy. The reason Frank was expected to decline the trip, or so we figured, was that through an unfortunate circumstance word had got abroad prematurely that I was pregnant.

"You certainly are going to take that cruise," I said when we discussed the matter, stubbornly resolved that no condition of mine should be the instrument of office finagling. "There's nothing you could do for me here, and things are going fairly smoothly as far as the household is concerned." That was so tenuous a circumstance that we both reached simultaneously for the nearest wooden object.

As a matter of fact at that moment we were wallowing in service. While nothing had ever really changed my opinion that Maria and Bandini were adequate help, particularly inasmuch as I had gradually taken on more and more jobs, still there came a time when I simply got tired of trying to cope with Maria's temperament and decided to get someone else to do it for me. We had hired a housekeeper, a foreign lady of impressive connections but impoverished circumstances, whose accomplishments in both English and Italian, and whose familiarity with Italian ways caused me to nourish the vain hope that my problems would be forthwith ended. Alas, I had underestimated the power of Maria for mischief and venom. My problems were not only not solved, they were augmented, for where I had previously parried only the maneuverings of Maria, I now found myself the mediator between Maria and Lina and was expected daily to sit in judgment as to which had insulted whom and to what extent.

All of this had undermined my morale to such an extent that when Lina had gone on a long visit to relatives, I had seized the opportunity to acquire the well-recommended maid of some departing American friends. And so we had Silvia.

Silvia had an unshakably serene disposition, a quiet competence, and a willingness to do more than her share of work, which temporarily mollified Maria, who was soon busily exploiting the situation to her own advantage.

Meanwhile I was a lady of leisure. I could stay in bed until noon if I chose, thus stalling off the twin devils of chill and nausea that dogged my footsteps when I arose. I had only to exert myself to the extent of lifting a hand to reach the buzzer if I wanted food or drink or a hot water bottle or just news of the household. It was as near to a perfect setup as one could wish to enjoy the beginning of the *stato interessante*, except that eventually one must arise and then all the king's horses and all the king's men could not have availed against the fire in the stomach and the chill in the bones.

And certainly there was nothing Frank could do except to offer moral support. So we decided he must take the trip, whereupon he was the object of as much envy as if he had just won twenty million in *totocalcio*. The Mediterranean in April! A deck to loll on under those lapis lazuli skies. Warmth. *O sole mio!*

The winter had been cold and wet, and in the cavernous, unheated and rain-dripping reaches of the old house we had all begun to have a slightly moldy outlook. There was simply no justice that Frank, and not I, should have this opportunity of escaping southward at that particular moment in history, but I was not exactly competent to cover the task force's maneuvers, and since the navy had so short-sightedly failed to invite wives of correspondents along, there was nothing for it but to bid Frank *buon viaggio* with the harrowing knowledge that he would be pretty much incommunicado for the next six weeks. He would let me know how to reach him in an emergency— but an EMERGENCY. Nothing trivial, you understand.

I was very brave and self-sacrificing until the jeep disappeared out the gate, and then I suddenly realized how big and empty the upstairs was going to be—I alone in my bedroom and Marta alone in hers. The heads of our beds touched opposite sides of the same wall, but the thickness of the wall was such that I had never yet been able to summon her by knocking on it or by shouting. I toyed with the idea of having her sleep with me and having Silvia sleep in her room instead of downstairs. Silvia was young, with a beautiful face and a gay laugh, and she was powerfully built. A veritable tower of strength from "high" Italy, so she seemed to me.

Silvia came up to bid me good night that first night. "*Signora,*" she said, "aren't you afraid to sleep up here alone?"

"What would I be afraid of?" I hedged, being unwilling to admit that I was, as a matter of cold fact, absolutely petrified whenever I thought how my windows and Marta's, as well as two of the salon windows, opened onto the flat tiled roofs which offered a continuous broad approach from the cluster of peasant houses at the other end of the property where, we knew, diverse black-market operations were carried on by night.

Silvia shrugged eloquently. "I would have too much fear," she said. She laughed musically and launched into an account of someone she had heard of being found murdered in bed.

"I'm sure I would wake up if anyone tried to break open the shutters," I said, being fully aware that if anyone *wanted* to break open the ancient, hinge-rusted contraptions he could do so easily. My tower of strength! I abandoned the idea of asking her to keep us company, and I refrained from mentioning that basement door which had been walled up after the motor had been stolen. I was pretty sure the "wall" that replaced the outer door could be pushed in with a casual elbow, being constructed according to the Italian formula of roughly one tablespoon of cement to a hundred pounds of garden dirt and having all the tensile strength of a mud-bee's nest. No use to alarm her by reminding her that her ground floor room, though just down the hall from the custodians' quarters, was right near that flimsy job of masonry.

Silvia had a fine collection of horror stories with which she regaled me. Seems she picked them out of the Rome daily papers, a source of terror hitherto not opened to me since my Italian was still too rudimentary to make reading a pleasure. We pooh-poohed them all quite merrily, and I traitorously labeled them "just newspaper stories." Still, it was no comfort to hear that an occupant of the Monte Farnesina caves had been rather intricately and fatally carved just the other night.

"*Buona notte, Signora,*" said my pillar of strength sweetly from the doorway. "*Buon riposo.*"

Buon riposo, indeed! I reached over and patted the handle of the thirty–eight Commando Special resting conveniently in one of my absent husband's old shoes under the edge of the bed. I had never even tried a practice shot with it and hoped to God I would never have to *hit* anything with it, but I did rather count on the terrible noise it would make if fired toward the ceiling being an effective deterrent should I hear any rattling of the shutters at night. But first I would always try to rouse Bandini by ringing the bell by my bed, for Bandini had assured me that *wh-i-sht* he would have on his pants in a minute and be at my side should there be the slightest noise.

I got through the first night, and several nights thereafter without incident if, indeed, without much sleep either. Then there came a night when something woke me sometime after midnight. I was at once alert. There came a sound at one of the shutters in the big salon. A softish knock, knock, and faint scratchings. Then silence. I sat up in bed and clutched the bell cord. The sound came again and I tried to listen above my wildly beating heart. Silence. If it comes once more, I decided, I'll ring for Bandini. It came again and I rang, praying that the current was on and the bell was functioning in the remote end of the house where Bandini was supposedly waiting with his pants at the fire-horse ready. Presently I heard his steps on the stairs and I relaxed against the pillow and began to breathe again.

When he came to my door I explained what I had heard. Clutching his Beretta, which was his contribution to the family arsenal, he made the rounds of the shutters, testing them. He looked out over the roof-tops. Nothing. He turned on the lights and looked for rats.

No rat. Presently he went on back downstairs and to bed murmuring that it was probably my imagination, I being in a *nervosa* state.

But I knew it was not my imagination and that there was no wind, and since nothing so steels my nerve as to be termed "*nervosa*," I determined that should the sound be repeated I would not call Bandini but would get up and have a look for myself. It came again after a while. I hesitated at the door, listening, trying to locate from which shutter the sound had come, then switched on the salon lights. There on the shutter clung a great locust struggling to escape, batting his inch-broad head against the wood and scrambling with his barbed drumstick legs.

I poured myself back into bed, relieved, and exonerated of Bandini's implication of female vapors.

Silvia always greeted me in the mornings with a faint air of surprise at finding my throat still intact. She always asked me if I had slept well. This morning I replied that I had slept very badly indeed. "I have heard a noise in the night," I said. "Tell Bandini that there *was* a noise, but it was nothing human—"

Silvia blanched. "Mother of God!" she said, and I realized that I had stirred her superstitious nature to its depths. "I mean," I said hastily, "that it was animal, *insect*." I did not know the word for locust but we went and found the creature on the window and released him outdoors, though I supposed in the interest of the farmers we should have killed him.

I did not know at that point, however, that it was not the lonely *nights* (while my husband cruised the Mediterranean presumably leaning over a rail and gazing at the silver moon-track across limpid waters), but the *days* which would be my real undoing.

The weather, after innumerable false promises, became suddenly warm and I dragged myself out into the morning sunshine with all the hopefulness of a reprieved convict emerging from his cell. I had settled back into a deck chair prepared to soak up the strength and heat of the fine, strong sun when I began to be assailed by a smell. The grape vines were blossoming over the trellis on the end of the terrace. White stars of jasmine in their glossy green foliage bedecked the weathered walls that glowed warm red-brown in the sun. Down the *viale* were great drifts of bridal wreath. What a world to be abroad in! But there was that smell. I thought irritably that the same cause which had turned the aroma of morning coffee into anathema had operated also on the scent of spring blossoms. I could not endure it. Reluctantly

I retreated into the cold interior of the house. Each morning I went hopefully out to the terrace and each morning was driven indoors shaking with nausea and disgust.

One morning, waking late and finding the sun already beating on the closed shutters of my room so that the warmth had penetrated even through the time-toasted wood, I knew that a day of intense heat was upon us. And everywhere, pressing in on me, was the scent. The odor. The stink! "It *can't* be the grape-blossoms," I said, reeling to the bathroom.

The bathroom was diagonally across the big salon from my room. We had had our supper in front of the fireplace the night before. Silvia had cleared away, but there on the little table for some unknown reason still stood the bowl of grape jelly. As I looked at it, the all-pervading odor seemed to be emanating like an invisible vapor from the bowl of jelly. Making a wide detour, I reached the bathroom. I got hold of myself after a while in the blue and white sanctuary of the big tiled bathroom and went back toward my own room.

"Of course it isn't the grape jelly," I told myself firmly. I walked over to it and smelled it boldly from close up. It had no smell at all that I could detect, except the faint, inoffensive, summery savor of preserved grape. Yet it seemed to glint malevolently at me and I set it hastily down.

When Silvia came up to bid me good morning, I removed the bed covers from my head and demanded, "What is that odor?"

Silvia sampled the atmosphere tentatively with her delicately chiseled nose. "What odor, *Signora?*" she asked.

I lay back with a wild sense of helpless frustration. Bandini thinks I hear sounds that don't exist. Silvia thinks I smell smells that don't exist. All that remains is to begin having visions. I thought of Frank stretched out in the inevitable position of sea-going relaxation on some air-washed deck and I began to wish I hadn't been so self-sacrificing about letting him go.

"Silvia," I began reasonably, "I seem to notice an odor and it is not a pleasant odor, and it gets worse every day. I don't *think* it is my imagination."

Silvia sniffed again. "Possibly," she admitted, "there is some little odor," and she used the word "*ambiente*" with a gesture toward the surrounding countryside as she opened the shutters and let in a flood of mote-filled sunshine.

Ambiente, I thought, trying out the unfamiliar Italian word but knowing what it meant and thinking "circumambient air" from some old poem. And then it dawned on me that this circumambient stink was probably coming up from the fields, some sort of fertilizer. I am a country girl and I think I recognize and have a certain respect for all known forms of fertilizer smells including aged sheep manure and some of the more offensive commercial brands. This did not fit into my previous experience with fertilizers.

"To me it smells like garbage," I said decisively, "*immondezza*."

"Ah, *si!*" exclaimed Silvia, comprehension wreathing her lovely face in a beatific light. "Ah, *si!* They fetch it from the city for the fields."

I recoiled in horror. "You don't mean to tell me the peasants are bringing city garbage out here to put on the fields!" I cried. "Besides, it wouldn't be any good," I insisted, trying to visualize the futility as well as the barbarity of strewing the fields with orange peel, scraps of paper and old potato parings, to mention the least obnoxious items.

"Not immediately on the fields, *Signora*," Silvia explained. "First they leave it a while to mature."

I lay back and gave over to the contemplation of the obscenity—city garbage "maturing" in the spring sunshine! Just then there was the sound of footsteps on the stairs and what I presumed to be Marta approaching my door. When I pulled myself up to look, however, the vision which met my eye confirmed all previous suspicions as to my wavering sanity. The creature in the doorway had great goggles for eyes in a grey, amorphous face with a dangling elephantine snout. The body was the body of my daughter, but the head was the head of—

"Look, Mommie," came a smothered sort of voice, "what we found on the garbage pile—a gas mask!"

"Oh," I gasped weakly with a dizzying kaleidoscopic blending of impressions, "well, thank you dear, maybe it would help, but—*where* did you say you found it?"

"On the garbage pile, the garbage *mountain*, Rita calls it."

Summoning my, by now, insane strength I rose from the bed. "Just where is this garbage mountain?" I thundered.

"Just outside our back gate in front of the peasants' house," Marta replied serenely in her underwater voice through the hose of the gas mask.

With an alacrity that belied my condition I ran through the salon, flung open the window of Marta's room and stepped through onto the terrace. Racing across to the edge of the terrace, I had a clear view of the surrounding houses and land. Sure enough, there was the garbage "mountain." At the foot of it crouched the old grandfather of the *contadini* family, gleaning happily. And up the road came another truckload. I watched fascinated as the truck backed up to the already enormous pile, reared back and deposited its dismaying contribution while all about me the sickish-sweet, corrupt odor defiled the sparkling air.

Back in my room I found myself alone with my helpless indignation. Marta and her treasure of a dirty gas mask had vanished to who knew what germ-laden haunt of childish fun. Silvia had gone about her household tasks. I began ringing all the bells I could find. Twice for Silvia, three times for Maria, enraged that I had no signal for Bandini and that anyway he was not on the premises during the daytime. Presently they converged upon me.

"Something has to be done about that garbage," I cried. "They *can't do* that. Surely it is a contravention of the laws of sanitation."

Maria and Silvia looked at each other and shrugged. "They do it every season, *Signora*," explained Maria. "It is the usual thing."

"But so close to a habitation," I insisted, "there must be a law."

"It is much closer to the house of the *contadini*," Maria explained reasonably, "than it is to *our* house, *Signora*."

Her unruffled calm enraged me. "Maybe *they* like it," I screamed. "Maybe it makes *them* happy to have garbage by their door but it does not make me happy and it is much too close to our house!"

It was not only my outraged sense of a public nuisance having been committed and the laws of sanitation flagrantly infringed right under my sensitive nose. Above all this rose the fighting spirit of my

Scottish ancestors at being thus robbed and cheated out of the full enjoyment of this country life so expensively bought and so precariously maintained. This was the season, and Italy the magnet, which drew countless numbers of retired English school teachers and congealed Scandinavians, not to mention poets, painters, and the jaded wealthy from all over the world.

Having endured a blistering Roman summer and a subhuman Roman winter in this house, was I now to be deprived of the indescribable joys of a Roman spring, locked up indoors with my nose swathed in bandages? I felt at the moment that nothing less than complete annihilation of those crude peasants, our neighbors, would do. I resented them and all their works, their mangy dogs and scabrous cats, their habit of squatting in our hedges or standing up in the full light of the sun beyond our archway and enhancing the morning with a urinal rainbow.

I was well aware that these Italian citizens with whom we shared a roof, though a blessedly extended one, were not the usual run of Italian farmers. They were some riff-raff who toyed at farming to cover a multitude of nefarious activities which included making black-market bread in the same hovel where luxuriated the pig.

How I despised them, and most of all for this final affront.

"Call the lawyer," I said in a flash of inspiration, remembering that Frank had left the lawyer's phone number in case of some emergency. "We pay an enormous lot of money for the privilege of living here," I said firmly, "and I do not intend to have to smell that garbage while it 'matures' for their miserable fields. Call the *avvocato* at once and tell him to come out and look into this offense."

It was plain that Maria and Silvia considered me *nervosa* but they flurried off reciting the number I gave them from my bedside list of important numbers to have at hand, including *carabinieri*, military police, doctors, lawyers, hospitals.

All the rest of the morning I paced the floor, the persistent stench of garbage penetrating even the closed windows and permeating the house. Whenever I crossed from my bedroom to the bathroom I gave a wide berth to the bowl of grape jelly, turning my head in order not to see the gunmetal glint of it there on the little center table. It never occurred to me simply to call Silvia and ask her to take it away, and as the day wore on and the *avvocato* could not be reached and the sound of trucks delivering more and more garbage reached even my shuttered rooms, the bowl of grape jelly, gleaming sullenly, seemed to epitomize the opaque, dark, cloying perversity of Italian life.

The lawyer was out of town. He would be back in a few days. *Pazienza, Signora.* Meanwhile the heat and the stench increased. There were cards from Frank. Crete was very interesting. The smells in Istanbul were out of this world. (Istanbul has nothing on us, I thought bitterly.) In case of an EMERGENCY you can reach me in care of U.S. Task Force, Carrier *Leyte*, Somewhere in the Mediterranean.

Bandini conveyed to me one morning the fascinating information that the garbage which the *contadini* were receiving was very special garbage. It was coming from the Polyclinic. Probably the Polyclinic's garbage is just like anybody else's garbage, but knowing the Italians' casual approach to matters of sanitation, this news of Bandini's opened new speculative vistas and put a more sinister edge to the now omnipresent smell.

"Have you spoken to them about the offense of this garbage?" I demanded of Bandini.

"*Sì, Signora*, I have spoken to them," replied Bandini, "but as you know I do not enjoy friendly relations with these *contadini* on account of their stealing of my garden water. They only reply that the *Signora* must be very *delicata* to object to the odor of garbage."

"Yes," I snorted, "I am *delicata*, Bandini. I am in fact the *principessa* who can feel the pea under the seven mattresses." We laughed ironically together for we both knew that by this time even the long-inured Bandini noses were beginning to resent the smell.

Three weeks of that lovely spring were history before what is technically known as an abatement took place. By this time the garbage mountain was so big that even though we had a court order for its removal it could obviously not be removed in any foreseeable future.

In the course of time the *avvocato* arrived, very continental and splendid as he lifted his moustache from the back of my hand and looked into my haggard eyes at short range with his exquisite, long-lashed black ones. "Do not disturb yourself, *Signora*," he murmured. "Leave everything to me."

After some negotiations at the house of the *contadini* which sounded, as I hopefully thought, as though he were beating them all to death, he returned as immaculate as ever to tell me that he had extracted a promise from the *padrone* of the garbage pile to put a layer of earth over it so that the *odore* could no longer escape. He recommended *pazienza*.

"A good thick layer of *terra*," I hoped, somewhat absently, for by that time a new crisis had arisen, a crisis which seemed to come almost under the category of EMERGENCY but of so delicate a nature that I could not—yet, at least—confide it even to this confidence-inspiring character, the *avvocato*.

This was the matter of the package for Catherine.

The office jeep-driver had brought me my mail daily, and this morning there had arrived a small package addressed to my husband in care of his office address and, in parentheses, "For Catherine." I racked my brains. I had never heard of any Catherine so far as I could remember, and wives have a fairly retentive memory for any female names their husbands happen to drop casually. I studied the small package, hefted it, rattled it, and tried to think whom it could possibly be for. In an agony of trepidation I poked into one end of the package hoping for some clue. To my utter confusion, the end of the box within bore the printed word "Insulin" and an expiration date, and the information that it had come from a London pharmacy.

Poor Catherine. Was she at this moment declining into a diabetic coma for lack of this little box of insulin, and what did my husband have to do with keeping her supplied with insulin, anyway? I began to wonder whether I shouldn't just laugh a fiendish laugh and dump it down the toilet and the hell with Catherine. Still, my better nature triumphed and I thought I ought to make some effort to locate Catherine. But how? Radio the Carrier *Leyte* Somewhere in the Mediterranean: "Who is Catherine?" I thought of inquiring at the office, casually, so as not to excite curiosity, "Say, do you happen to know a girl named Catherine?" But reflecting that probably everyone (except me) knows a girl named Catherine, and that office males have a notable solidarity about covering up for each other, I abandoned it as fruitless. After all, my husband and I had been separated for years by the war and you never could tell. But there *he* was lolling on some deck and having a wonderful time, and I should be worrying about Catherine!

While I was worrying, the expiration date on the box came and went and I supposed there was nothing further I could do about saving—or scuttling—poor Catherine. So I put the box aside and looked forward with a certain malevolency to confronting my husband with it when he should come home all brown and relaxed from his cruise.

Eventually—*years* after he had departed that day in April, the six weeks were finally up and he came home. I was so glad to see him and the usual plunder collected on such a journalistic junket, that it wasn't for some moments that I remembered to bring out the box for Catherine.

Frank looked at it in obvious bewilderment. "*Cath*erine," he said frowning, "who the devil is Catherine?"

"That's what I wondered," I said in a small voice.

Then he remembered. Oh yes, Catherine Somebody or other, Polish name. Used to come into the office. Displaced person living in some camp. Asked if she could have some packages sent her in care of the office address because certain things aren't supposed to be received by displaced persons. *Months* since she had been heard from. Wouldn't even know where to locate her now. Throw the damn stuff away. She intended selling it on the black market, obviously.

"Well," I said, more relieved than I cared to have him see, "all kinds of things were going on up here while you were lolling around on the deck of that carrier."

"Listen," he interrupted, "did you ever *see* the deck of a carrier? Looks enormous, all right, but there isn't an inch allotted for 'lolling' as you put it. I've got a bad case of claustrophobia from being almost the entire six weeks shut up below decks in a boiler factory."

I hope, as the one who always stays home, that I didn't take too much satisfaction from noting at this point that my husband's sea-going complexion was almost as sallow as my own.

12

Haunted By the Count

Given the same number of inhabitants—four, say, or five—housekeeping problems in twenty rooms are not four times greater than in five rooms. This is a mathematical anomaly which seemed incomprehensible to most of our friends who lived in apartments while we rattled around in the villa.

"Heavens," they would say, "you must have to have a staff!"

Maria shared this delusion with respect to the big house. Graduated from four tiny rooms jam-packed with relatives, the villa seemed to her like an immensity which could only be kept in order by superhuman effort on the part of five or six servants. The idea that she and her husband and the laundress were to be the only help in a house of such proportions was a continuous affront to the sensibilities of Maria.

I suppose if there had been ten in our family and we had gone in for large-scale entertaining, her grievance would have been justified. As it was, there were only two bedrooms to be made up, one bathroom to clean, one dining room and one living room to be put in order daily. The rest of the house was so little "lived in" that it scarcely counted. Much of the space in a big house is show-space, so to speak. Nothing much happens in it. Nothing moves. Nothing is displaced. A dusting now and then is about all it requires. For state occasions you polish the furniture and beat the rugs, but otherwise it just reposes.

The battle against clutter which all housewives are familiar with and wage ceaselessly from the altar to the grave goes on much more intensively in a small house than in a large one. A peasant's bed in which sleep two to five people has to be "broken" as they say, and the bedding hung out to be aired every day. Floors of two or three little rooms across which tramp half a dozen people of miscellaneous ages, dropping crumbs and spilling things and tossing down their cigarette butts, naturally have to be mopped daily. But in a big place where the traffic is lighter much of this daily cleaning is pointless, a proposition which is only conveyed to an Italian maid with the greatest of patience and at the risk of discouraging her from ever mopping the floor again.

Having had, from infancy, an allergy to spring and fall housecleaning time when everything was turned upside down and hung out and beaten, I was appalled to discover in Italy that the process went on every day, and every day you had a sense of being ousted from the quiet precincts of your home while beds were hung over balconies, chairs were upended, floors were mopped and feather dusters were whisked relentlessly about your very ears.

Nor did all this disturbance necessarily imply great cleanliness. The feather dusting was a sort of symbolic ritual which missed most of the surfaces. The mopping scarcely ever reached into corners and left the rooms reeking either of chlorine bleach or the faint, fetid odor of a dirty mop cloth.

I taught Maria how to make up the beds without hanging everything out to air more than twice a week, how to dust thoroughly and to mop even into the corners with a clean cloth and soapsuds on her once-a-week cleaning day instead of the usual daily wipe-up that hit only the easily accessible parts of the floor. The household began to run with a minimum of disturbance and effort, and the sound of the beating of rugs that echoes up and down Italy from dawn to dusk was heard no more—not from our house at least—after ten a.m.

The House of the Four Winds took on a new tranquility and you could be sure—well, almost sure—that if you sat down in the sun on the terrace no one would shake a dust-cloth or empty the ashtrays on you from the window above.

The saving of time and effort effected by a few simple housekeeping shortcuts proved somewhat embarrassing to Maria's campaign for extra help in the house, but her fixation upon the subject was profound and not to be shaken by anything so trivial as the fact that another maid would have been pure luxury. There was, also, the matter of "face," as I was to discover one day when I was outlining a menu with Maria in anticipation of some guests that evening, and found her scowling and irritable.

"What is the matter?" I interrupted to inquire.

"*Signora*, excuse me," said Maria, "but it is impossible to make a *bella figura* in this house without at least one maid. Now the Count…"

Oh yes, the Count! So that was what stood between me and Maria, the shadow of the Count. This gentleman, I knew from her earlier reports of him, had looked at the villa before we came along and leased it. He had contemplated renting it himself and cutting, I suppose, a very *bella figura* all around. At least that was the impression he had given to Maria, and he had assured her that should he decide to honor the villa with his presence she would be put in charge of a staff of domestics ranging from personal maids to doormen.

The Count had opened up fantastic vistas in the mind of Maria, but these *Americanini*, on the other hand, these little Americans, had no sense of the beautiful life. Under their system Maria was turning out to be merely a maid, a *tuttofare* even, and not the chatelaine she would like to have been, the *Signora* of the kitchen.

The fact that the Count had found the rent exorbitant and had had to look elsewhere for a house in which to carry on his beautiful life was immaterial, as was also the fact that he might very probably have rationed second-rate spaghetti to his staff. Still, he had *said*...

"Maria," I said firmly, "we have no intention of living as the Count would like to live—if he could afford it. We live simply and we do not entertain on the grand scale. These guests who are coming are Americans not yet six months in Italy. They will not be interested— yet—in a *bella figura*. See that the meat is tender. I myself may even pass the potatoes."

Maria was impressed, but adversely. She withdrew grumblingly from my presence and went back to the kitchen. And with her, down the staircase, went our personal poltergeist, the gaunt, decadent, perfumed, and slightly frayed figure of the Count.

And he was lurking around the house in unexpected places. He was there, looking over my shoulder when I scoured out the bathtub. He sneered down his finely chiseled nose when I essayed to light the fire in the fireplace instead of calling Bandini to do it for me.

Even in the garden where coffers of splendid jewels were bursting in the Italian sun, each in its season—pearls of cauliflower gleaming from their green sheaths, emeralds of broccoli Romani, many faceted (a vegetable too beautiful to be true, like a tiny conventionalized Christmas tree, and unknown to American gardens), the coral of beans, the jade of zucchini, the ruby of tomatoes, the deep rich amethyst of eggplant—I would have liked nothing better than to weed and water and pick. But was that the hand of the Count on my wrist when I reached for a rake?

I began belatedly to give more thought to the problem of becoming a lady. I gave in, almost imperceptibly it is true, to the superior forces of tradition and position, especially after one harrowing experience where we essayed an American picnic-type luncheon under the trees in the courtyard and found our American friends already so stratified that they stood around waiting for our non-existent "staff" to bring chairs from the house, when I had innocently assumed that of course everyone would pitch in and help, just as we had always done at home.

My hapless solution to Maria's repeated appeals for assistance was to hire a cleaning woman to take over the heavy work. We had always had the laundress, a statuesque young woman who walked up a steep trail from her home in a cave in the Farnesini hills. (The Bandini laundry as well as our own was done by this girl, a process which Maria directed, keeping the accounts as well—a custom which had been established before I came, and went on until Lina, as housekeeper, discovered that the Bandini laundry was always done first and that our tablecloths and tea towels were very likely to be washed out after the Bandini underwear. It was by her reporting of this interesting arrangement that Lina had earned the undying hatred of Maria and had been the recipient of some of her most lurid abuse.)

Now, to Maria, who was very *brava* in preparing the wonderful garden vegetables, in making ravioli and other Italian delicacies, I would turn back all of the cooking, much of which I had been doing myself, while I intended to devote myself to the gentler arts of photography or even writing. It was about time I began to commit some of my immortal thoughts to paper. Wouldn't hurt me to stay in bed later mornings, either, and get in a few sun-baths.

For some months after the advent of Assunta, blue-eyed, gentle, slow, and thorough, both Maria and the spirit of the Count were exorcised, and I complimented myself on how well I managed things. With my remarkable capacity for missing the point, however, it did not dawn upon me until many scenes and much bloodshed later that what Maria wanted was not more help but total retirement from domestic service.

Before long the house began to reverberate again with the voice of Maria, a veritable cataract of sound, haranguing her child or her patient husband over some minor offense. Bandini took every slightest occasion to open a conversation with us which always got around sooner or later to an encomium of his wife, how good she was, how patient, how honest. She was also, however, very "*nervosa.*"

"She should learn to control her temper," I told him. "I do not like such yelling in the house."

Bandini was apologetic but firm in his defense of Maria's character. The trouble was, he explained, she worked too hard and she was not really of the servant class. Were we not considering getting a maid? We were not. If the Bandinis were not satisfied with the situation as it existed, they were quite free to go elsewhere.

That, however, was not what they had in mind. They regarded themselves as fixtures in the house. The *padrone* had assured them it was agreed in the contract that they were to be the permanent "custodians." We, too, were under the impression that we could not dispense with their services. Therefore we parried the approaches for more help, bore as well as we could the sulkings of Maria, and two or three times a week engaged in full-scale argument from which I always emerged shaken with the suspicion that, whereas I had intended to describe in forceful and convincing style the extent of our bounty in providing quarters, utilities, garden, and incidentals too numerous to mention with a scathing summation of the Bandinis' lack of appreciation, I had, instead, merely sputtered ineffectually in laughably fractured phrases.

Psychologists to the contrary, who place "security" high on the list of factors contributing to stability of character, we began to believe that Maria was suffering the effects of too much security. When she had had to share the crowded quarters of relatives during the war years, putting up with all sorts of inconveniences and difficulties, she was undoubtedly a sweeter and more cooperative character, for nothing guaranteed her continued hospitality except her ability to get along amicably and pull her own weight. One temper tantrum in the presence of mother-in-law such as she threw daily in our kitchen would probably have resulted in her being invited to go live somewhere else.

Things were different now. Under the magic protection of a "contract" which seemed to assure her of a roof over her head regardless of how much or how little she contributed to the household, all her native unpleasantness began to assert itself.

Maria suffered from two quite understandable but equally unrealizable ambitions: she wanted a home of her own, or lacking that, a Signorial position in whatever house she happened to dwell in, and she wanted another child. In the former she was frustrated by our persistent reluctance to increase our already heavy financial burden by hiring a "staff" for her to supervise. In the latter we seemed to be cooperating with divine providence in preventing her from having another child.

This desire for a son and heir was an obsession with her, but some constitutional weakness or anatomical disability made conception difficult and she spent most of her waking hours consulting with neighbor women, village midwives and, when she could afford it, doctors. Her most recent advice was to the effect that she should spend a good part of each month in bed in order to facilitate the desired end. If this did not bring results, then an operation was advised.

Under the circumstances—and it may be a proof of the inhumanity Maria attributed to us—we admitted to being not too sympathetic with Maria's ambitions toward augmenting the race. With one child already for whom it was a real sacrifice for them to buy clothes, school books, and medical care, it seemed to us very considerate indeed of nature to have offered her a simple means of limiting her family. I shuddered at the prospect of a pregnant Maria (though it might have transformed her into a creature of sweetness and light), and I took an equally dim view of the possibility of a squalling infant in the lower regions of the house.

While we gave in, now and then, by hiring a housekeeper or a maid, we persisted in our refusal to relieve Maria entirely of her responsibilities and leave her free to recline in bed awaiting the working out of her desires. So poor Maria fretted, brooded, and raged by turns. Still, she went quietly ahead with her plans to improve on nature. Without taking us into her confidence she had arranged to take time off and have the operation. A couple of months to build up her strength beforehand, a couple of months to recuperate afterward. And who knew what after that—nine months of pampering herself? Not at our expense, we grimly decided. It was time to consult the lawyer again.

"Give them notice," the lawyer said briskly.

"But the contract...?"

"The contract! You know I went all over that contract and had it redrawn sensibly," he said. "You have no obligations regarding the custodians whatever. They are one of the clauses I had deleted."

What news! And how stupid of us not to have read over the new contract in the light of our developing troubles. We waited for the next scene and then we broke it to them.

"Not in the contract!" Bandini was scornful. The *padrone* had assured him... He would go and inform himself. He came back next afternoon from his excursion into Rome to the office of the landlord, meek as a lamb. Alas, it was all too true. "*Signore*," he said respectfully, "What do you wish us to do?"

We thought likely, since so many insults had been exchanged under the protection of the contract, that it would be best for all concerned if we parted company. At long last we were able to provide Maria with the leisure she wanted to devote herself to higher things— though not exactly on the terms she had hoped for.

When I saw the last of the Bandini furniture being carted down the driveway followed by the squat form of Maria, I had the unmistakable impression that another shadowy figure marched beside her. At least from that moment I was never again troubled by the specter of the Count.

13

A Good Safe Place

The first time I saw my Roman-born baby, her hair was standing on end just as I expected it would be.

It was probably that last nocturnal disturbance that did it, although previously at regular intervals during those months when serenity is generally indicated, there had been enough incidents of one sort or another to have given her a permanent pompadour. Always before, though, there had been a man around the place and it had never previously devolved upon me to shoulder a weapon and prepare to defend my home and honor.

Frank was working nights. The custodians had been invited to pack up their kitchen pans, their personal effects, their problems, and their complaints and take themselves elsewhere, so we no longer had the doubtful security of the presence of Bandini. Of the various other men we had interviewed or tried out for the job, none had proven satisfactory. So there remained Lina the housekeeper, Marta, and I to man the manless ramparts.

Lina had come into our lives when, after nearly a year at the villa, our relations with the Bandinis had reached such an impasse that I felt I could no longer cope with the situation alone. A housekeeper seemed like a good solution, especially one who, according to some third hand information from friends of people who had employed her, spoke both English and Italian and had been long enough in Italy to know all the angles, oblique and obtuse as they were, in Italian living. I was quite ready to hand over my authority as the *Signora*, together with the responsibility of settling arguments and laying down the law.

Lina, so we heard, could "do anything," was willing to work like a bird-dog, but she didn't wish to be treated like a servant for she had known better days. That was all right. We, being American, had the traditional light hand with the help, in fact most of our troubles stemmed from this virtue or weakness depending upon the point of view, and I felt I could meet Lina's requirement without too much trouble if she were the priceless jewel she was reputed to be.

I remember the morning I went to the front gate to let Lina in for our first interview. It was in September but still very warm. She was dressed in a simple white cotton frock, her yellow hair was done neat and high, her smile was friendly. She was such a contrast to the squat, black-smocked, stringy-haired, broad-beamed domestic type that I was ready to take her on sight. She seemed exactly the kind of person who could take over my wobbly household and put it on its feet. Her English seemed adequate. I explained the set-up, and she fell in love with the villa at once and was not even averse to having a six-year-old girl around. She made her decision to come to us without taking the thinking over period I had suggested.

"I *must* work," she said, with an emphasis which I thought meant that she was destitute but which later I found to have quite other implications.

So Lina came to live with us and was pleased with the big room on the ground floor with long windows looking out into the wheat fields and toward the blue hills beyond. She came with a simple old battered suitcase and said that her "things" would be sent later.

But when her things arrived, they arrived in a truck and there were four trunks full. Out of the trunks she lifted evening dresses, suits, silver fox furs, a Persian lamb coat, an ermine wrap. When I came upon her unpacking with these items laid across the bed, my eyes popped. "But you have such beautiful things!" I said.

"They are out of style," Lina replied sadly. "I *had* beautiful things, and perhaps this Persian can be remodeled."

She groped among the trunk trays and brought forth an album containing pictures of the home she had once had before the death of her husband. It was sumptuous, period furniture and damask covered walls. I began to have qualms about this person I had hired to take over the housework.

"No, no!" she protested when I suggested that perhaps we had made a mistake. "I can do everything. I no longer have these fine things and I am not like these Italian Signoras, I am not afraid to work. I am proud to work."

We left it at that, but on her first afternoon off when she made up her face with the touch of an artist, dressed in her plum-colored tailleur and set a smart hat on her trim coiffure—be-veiled and be-gloved, she was as stunning a figure as might cross the Excelsior lobby any afternoon at five. As a matter of fact she was bound for the Excelsior lobby. I was totally out-Ritzed.

When, a few weeks after her arrival, Lina informed me that she was buying a house in Rome, I decided our wires must have been crossed somewhere. "But didn't you say you had to work for a living?" I asked incredulously.

"I *must* work," she repeated as on the first day, "otherwise I go mad." She explained that the death of her husband, and before that the death of her only child, coupled with the loss of her home and her wealth, had laid a compulsion of activity upon her, but as for money, that was an indifferent matter. She still had some interests in her husband's properties which now and then brought her in a good piece of cash.

My doubts increased as to the practicality of having as a housekeeper the widow of a well-to-do shipping magnate of Naples, especially since her position as overseer of the household was seriously compromised by the necessity for her to do the upstairs cleaning. Lina's English, while strange, had seemed adequate. But on her first day in the house it was evident that she either had not understood or had not listened to my explanation of the situation regarding Maria, namely that Maria considered herself a superior being, wife of the "custodian," whose position was established by contract and who no longer would condescend to do anything except the cooking and maintaining the kitchen end of the house—and that only because, as she frequently pointed out, she was a very good-hearted person.

Lina made the initial error on her first day by asking Maria to do some job. Maria exploded so violently and with such tremendous reverberations, that Lina was made fully aware—in Italian with a French accent—that Maria was nobody's "maid." When she came to me for confirmation of this disconcerting fact, I offered Lina a chance to withdraw from her bargain in light of her new understanding. But Lina was in that well-known state of mind of the bereaved when any new blow is accepted—perhaps welcomed—as a further confirmation of her status vis-à-vis destiny. She thought for a few moments. Drew herself up dramatically and repeated, "*I* am not afraid of work!"

Thereafter Lina was a dynamo of energy and took, I thought, a morbid pleasure in doing menial work such as mopping floors and beating rugs. I had pleaded with her daily to skip some of the mopping and dusting but to no avail. She only tore into it with renewed vigor.

But in the afternoons and evenings she went forth, a model of sartorial perfection beside which I in my bargain basement wardrobe was definitely dowdy.

After the arrival of Lina our telephone began to get a workout such as it had not had during our unsocial months at the villa. When she was out I became a sort of secretary keeping track of her calls from real estate agents, dressmakers, Roman friends. Often she came home at midnight on the dingy tram wearing her finery which included a string of real pearls and some enormous rings, and until I heard her enter the side door I was always uneasy for her welfare. Then there was the matter of her keeping her furs and silver in her bedroom which was on the ground floor and easily accessible to prowlers should the windows not be locked. She was inclined to pooh-pooh the necessity but after considerable urging and the mysterious disappearance of a sheet and her own nightgown which had been left over a chair near the open window to air one morning, she was persuaded to store her things of value in the inside storeroom.

By this time the things of value included not only her own set of sterling flatware and odd platters and bowls, but a set of a dozen hand-wrought silver plates she had had made for some wealthy relative. All these we had prevailed upon her to put safely away behind several locked doors. But now and then a ship of her late husband's line would dock in Naples and she would come into a small fortune in a percentage of its cargo. Not knowing where else to invest her money, she would buy a kilogram—something over two pounds—of gold. This costly bar she would stow away in her bank. Between its purchase, however, and her trip to the bank there would often be a lapse of time during which the bar would be in the house and I would be on pins and needles until she removed it. She gave up telling me, after a while, when she came home with a kilo of gold in her little round muff, and I gave up reminding her about the vulnerability of her own room, for by then I was pregnant and had problems of my own.

Not that the presence of Lina had ever greatly minimized my problems. She was a sensitive soul and I a notoriously cold and matter-of-fact character. I was able to treat her as a member of the family but more as a respected aunt than the kissin' cousin she would like to have been to all of us. I was constantly failing to show the required amount of enthusiasm for some small favor or special dish, and I would find myself confronted by wounded silence or even tears.

Anyone less green than I in the delicate relationship between the classes in Italy would have known that Lina's innate aristocratic air and the necessity in our household that she do some of the actual work were too incongruous to be understood by the Bandinis. Lina was both too much a lady and too efficient a worker, and Maria couldn't stomach it, for how can you respect a *Signora* who mops the floors, especially when she mops them better than you do and thus usurps the ancient privilege of the laboring class? So Maria hurled defiance at Lina and Lina bore it as a further evidence of her martyrdom, and I found myself daily salving the pride and wounded feelings of each. I began to wonder what had happened to the time-honored prerogative of the *pregnant* woman to be temperamental.

Withal, I was not a little relieved when Lina decided to make her annual trip up the continent to visit relatives. Silvia came along fortuitously then, and there was a definite satisfaction in having a simple country girl around the place whose *amour propre* couldn't be dented with a pickax, and to whom my modest wardrobe still looked good enough to class *me* as the *Signora* of the house.

I played the *Signora* angle for all I could get out of it for the next few months and would probably have enjoyed the early part of my *stato interessante* in such luxury as I had never previously known had not the new girl, Silvia, been so kind-hearted and efficient that Maria, also, decided to take things easy.

Confiding only in Silvia, Maria planned herself a good long vacation in the mountains for August. Silvia agreed it would be a beautiful thing, but she quietly made her own plans to leave just about that time, for it was obvious that she would be stuck with all the work.

Even the fact that Maria's vacation coincided with our own did not deter Maria. Listing all the urgencies which develop around the activities of the servant class, her vacation could not be postponed. We decided about this time to have a final reckoning with our "custodians" whom we had been housing, feeding, and to a large extent clothing over the course of our tenancy of the house in exchange for an ever-diminishing amount of part-time work. It ended with Maria getting her vacation, all right, a permanent one, and with our staying home to look after the house which, according to the contract, could never be left without someone to guard it.

While we were thus engaged in babysitting the house, we enjoyed our most tranquil week to date. If there were no servants, there were also no arguments. If the dust accumulated under the beds and the floors went temporarily unmopped, at least we had peace and we "ate American," which was a pleasant change. And then, out of the blue, Lina came back.

This was a blessing, but not unmixed.

The idea of "buying a house" had developed into a project of building an apartment. This involved endless conferences with architects and workmen, and endless imbroglios with lawyers and engineers. The thing was costing more and more, and Lina was getting more and more desperate as it neared completion. Though she could cook very well when she put her mind to it, with her various outside activities she had become phenomenally preoccupied and vague, and she was more absent than present in our household during the day.

Lina arranged, however, always to be home at night since Frank's work required him to be down in the city from dusk to dawn. When he left in the evening we locked up the house and shuttered the windows and pulled down the iron doors. There was a great deal of bolting and barring to be done every night, and it somehow all added to, rather than diminishing, our sense of insecurity. Lina would retire to her downstairs room and Marta and I would go upstairs to our respective beds. In the morning Frank would come home, but there were long, dark, sound-filled nights to be got through. I was by this time well along with my epic project of perpetuating the race, and when I went to bed with the gun in the shoe beside me, I hoped nothing would transpire that would deprive me of my well-earned rest for at least eight hours.

It seemed to me that I had barely said good night to Lina, that night, tucked Marta into her bed in the room adjacent to mine, and gone to bed and to sleep before I heard Lina again at my door. It was midnight, however, and she said in her calm, rather tired voice, "There is someone trying to get into my room."

"How do you mean?" I asked. "Are you sure?" I had a feeling she might be imagining it.

"Yes," she insisted. "There is a pushing at my shutters and you can see that they move."

"Is your light on?" I asked. Yes, she had turned on the light but the rattling had persisted. This sounded bad. Evidently, then, it was someone who was indifferent to the fact that the room was occupied, someone who knew that the custodians were no longer with us, that the *padrone* was away for the night, and that the women could be taken care of easily once he got inside.

There was nothing for me to do but to put on a bathrobe and slippers, pick up the gun—a great, big, heavy revolver that I could barely carry in one hand—and accompany Lina back downstairs. I hadn't stopped to figure out a plan of campaign. I guess it just seemed better to try to foil an entrance than to cope with some tough character after he had got in.

It was with the fatalistic sort of false courage my year in the villa had engendered that I crept down the dim stairway ahead of Lina, fully expecting that the shutters might already have given way and I might encounter someone at any turning. I was sick with the certainty that here, at last, was the moment in which I would have to "shoot it out" with some desperado. The house had been entered before, there was no reason to doubt that it would be again. But strangely enough, the thing that bothered me most at the crucial moment was not whether, if necessary, I would remember how to fire the gun, but what in God's name I was going to *say* before I fired. You don't just shoot a person, even a burglar, do you, without giving him some warning? And in *Italian!*

Nothing in my sixty-four-dollar record course, my year of domestic problems or social chit-chat had helped my vocabulary in this direction. How I wished I had rehearsed some appropriate phrase like, "Stop, I have a gun here! I'll shoot!"

By the time we reached the lower landing I had remembered that the Italian word for gun is *fucile* but for the life of me I couldn't think where to put the accent.

By the time we reached the entrance hall I began to hope I would be spared the embarrassment of addressing an unknown Italian in the wrong tense. There was no sound in the entrance hall except the sudden and reassuring cuck-ing of the cuckoo-clock.

We proceeded down the back hall and toward the door of Lina's room, and as we did so the feeble light she had left burning went out. I choked down another golf ball trying to convince myself that it was just a routine current failure and we went on. I stuck the gun and one eye around the corner of the door and Lina played the flashlight about the room. Nothing. We went inside and examined the windows, but not too minutely. The shutters seemed intact. I drew about a quarter of a breath and said, "Maybe you were dreaming."

Lina was indignant in a mild way. "I had not yet gone to bed," she said. "I had been reading in the dining room when I heard the noise." She insisted there had been a definite pushing and rattling of the shutters. Remembering that earlier attempt on the studio door, I had no reason to doubt her word but neither did I have any intention of exploring the matter further.

"Oh, well," I said, "let's lock your door from the outside, call up Frank in Rome, and then go upstairs to wait. Whoever is trying to get in would still have to break through the door to get into the rest of the house."

Lina agreed it seemed sensible, but she was hesitating.

"You don't have anything valuable in your room, anyway," I urged, remembering that she had complied with our insistence that her valuables be stored elsewhere.

"Well," she admitted sheepishly, "I *do* have a kilo of gold in here somewhere."

"A kilo of gold!" I hissed. "But we *warned* you..!" She groped briefly in the wardrobe and rummaged in the bureau drawers. "Oh, let it go," she said at last, and it did seem to me she deserved to lose it.

We went out of her room and locked the door, and I hurried to the telephone. Frank would come at once, but the drive up from Rome would take at least twenty minutes. "Sit tight," he advised, "and keep the gun on you."

To be nearer Marta and further from the room of Lina, we went upstairs and sat down in the big salon, I with the weapon in what was left of my lap. It was not until much later that I was able to laugh every time I thought of myself descending the staircase with that terrible gun dragging down my right shoulder, my bathrobe clutched about my bulging middle. Had I met a burglar he would probably have died laughing.

We heard the jeep in the courtyard after what seemed an eternity, and we went downstairs to open up the iron door for Frank and the Italian driver. Together they did a quick tour all around the ground floor inside to see that the doors and shutters were all intact. As they stood in the darkness just inside Lina's door wondering what to do next, suddenly there was a stirring, sighing sound outside the windows. Lina and I froze to the door-frame just outside the room while Frank and the driver, armed to the teeth, went quickly and threw open the shutters.

Transfixed in the ring of light from the flashlight was a dark, bearded face with unblinking eyes. It was the face of the neighboring peasants' black goat, and she gave us all a reproachful look as she hopped down from the window ledge where she had been comfortably bedded for the night.

"I just remember where I put that kilo of gold," Lina murmured at this point. "I brought it home in my muff yesterday and left it right here so I would not forget to put it in a good safe place."

She picked it up off the bureau where it had been lying in plain sight, wrapped in a bit of old newspaper. Beside it were her platinum watch, her pearl necklace, and a massive gold bracelet elaborately wrought.

14

Battle Jackets in the Delivery Room

She was to have been called Peter, being born in Rome. But being a girl, and tiny, she became Pebble instead.

The austere conventions of birth- and baptism-certificates, however, do not accede to any such whimsicality in naming a young Christian, so she has other names as well. The first, to commemorate her Roman heritage, is Prassede after the girl in early Christian literature (also called Praxedis) whose family gave shelter to Saint Peter in ancient Rome, and whose church in the Eternal City, in the shadow of Saint Mary Major, is one of the oldest and loveliest. The second name is Elizabeth as a conventional leaven.

When her birth was imminent, Lina was in the throes of another form of creation—the building of an apartment—and the attendant pangs, faithfully transmitted to me through Lina, were such that I came to feel at times that I might possibly be giving birth to a house instead of a child.

Lina's "house" began to be built about the time the Pebble was conceived. As her birth approached, the activities regarding the construction were mounting to a new crescendo, the climax of which was the delivery into Lina's hands of the plaster-wet, paint-sweet apartment. It was unfortunate that the delivery of the house was premature, or at least preceded by two weeks the delivery of Pebble. For at this critical point, Lina must without delay make a trip to Naples to get her furniture to be moved into the new house.

The birth, according to the doctor, was due on the 13th of November. But Lina, being long associated with Italian signs and superstitions, had decided that it could not possibly occur before the 25th. Hence she had a leeway of time during which she could go to Naples, collect her furniture, and return to Rome.

I did not share her faith in signs. I inclined to take the doctor's word for it, but Lina was not to be deterred. She seemed impelled by demonic haste to get the furniture, already six years in storage, in place in the still-damp apartment. "I will be back when you need me," she said with assurance as she departed.

I took the precaution, however, of arranging for other help. Our cleaning woman had a friend who needed a job, and so Elettra came into our lives. Elettra had a deep, husky, impelling voice and a habit of saying "*Signora mia*" in an irresistible way—the way, I later discovered, it is murmured into every passing ear by the mammas of six children who make their living by begging on the streets. But Elettra was not one of these. She was the widow of a tailor and she had two children, one girl fourteen years old who lived with her, and one about eight who was "backward" as a result of the *bombardimento*, so they said, and had been placed in a *collegio* at some distance from Rome.

Elettra had never worked as a domestic, and her primitive life in her Abbruzzi mountain home had not instructed her in the conventions. When she consulted with me, she drew up a chair intimately near mine and, resting her chin on her clasped hands, addressed me familiarly. I found it rather an endearing habit, and I liked to look at her fine-boned face set off by a bright scarf knotted gypsy-fashion under one ear.

She had a room in the village at an infinitesimal blocked rental and for this reason Elettra was reluctant to "live in" at the villa. Absence from the room at night, she claimed, would establish it as uninhabited and risk the owner's reclaiming it. So we arranged that she could go home at night except for the time when I would be in the hospital, when she would have to sleep in the villa. She and her daughter and their friend, the cleaning woman, played about with the work and seemed very happy, and I paid little attention to how they did it, preferring to keep out of the kitchen and not tangle with them over any little faults until after the baby was born and I could take the household in hand again.

Armistice Day in 1947 was a day of tranquil loveliness. Late roses still bloomed in the garden. A few fall rains had replenished the green. The sun fell in a benediction of honey-colored light across the courtyard and through the leaf-lightened arbors where the vine we call Virginia creeper and the Italians call Canadian creeper, had already turned crimson. I was out all day in the courtyard and the garden and I guessed by the surge of energy I felt that this would probably be the day. I only hoped when the time came that the car would start and we would get in to the Clinic in Rome without incident.

We had barely got comfortably settled for the night when I got an unmistakable tip-off that the time had come to get to the Clinic. My doctor was an army doctor, but the army hospital had recently been closed and his practice was now taken to an Italian clinic.

It was just midnight when we rolled the car out of the front room into the courtyard. By great good fortune this was not one of its temperamental nights and the starter worked like a charm. Elettra came out into the yard where the moon laid its milk-white light, eerily illuminating the familiar courtyard and casting intense shadows from the mulberry and bay trees.

"*Stia tranquilla*," said Elettra, "I will attend to everything."

The drive from Monte Mario into Rome at night is one of the world's memorable sights. Monte Mario is considerably higher than the fabled seven hills of the ancient city, which are actually only minor elevations. The road winds along the edge of the highlands and descends tortuously, a road called *Trionfale*—the triumphal way. Spread below in the great basin of the Tiber valley twinkle the lights of Rome, a sea of stars with the moon-blanched dome of St. Peter's islanded among them.

We slowed to a stop at the crest, where the shadow of the Vatican observatory spills over into the valley, for a better view—and then plunged downward into this bowl of stars and all the unknown quantities that awaited us in the sleeping and somewhat sinister city. For those were still the days when cars could not be parked unattended in the streets.

We found the Clinic and parked in front of it, as there was no courtyard in which the car could be left. There were no attendants to watch it, and for the moment there was nothing to be done but for me to take my little bag and go alone into the hospital while Frank sought a safe place for the car.

A nun opened the door for me, conducted me down a hall to the elevator, and finally to a room. There an English-speaking nurse took me over. "I have called the doctor," she said, "and he is coming right over though I told him it was *much* too early and he might just as well sleep awhile."

You and your Italian intuition, I thought, I don't think it is much too early. It so happens I am a fast worker in these matters.

I was delighted to see the doctor a short while later, a great, big, young blond American with beautiful teeth and the open, corn-fed look and faultlessly pressed uniform that so distinguished American army men among the Italians in those days.

"What has become of my husband?" I asked, since Frank had not yet come into the hospital. The doctor laughed. "He's sitting in my car parked behind yours, holding my gun," he said. "We've sent for an attendant but until he gets here somebody has to watch the cars."

The doctor stood above me with some medicine in his hand. "Are you allergic to anything?" he asked.

"Me?—No!" I replied boastfully. "Not a thing. You take my husband now..." I was about to regale him with stories of Frank's spectacular allergic reactions to all kinds of innocent things like aspirin and whiskey, but he stopped me short by popping a capsule of something called Seconal into my mouth. Then he vanished to get scrubbed.

A few minutes later, fate took what I have always regarded as a rather underhanded way of rebuking me for laughing at my husband's frailties. The Seconal was returned violently via the route it had taken and I, who had never previously been allergic to anything, discovered I had an allergy. My tongue, throat, and nasal passages promptly swelled nearly shut. I could scarcely breathe and could not talk. A fine state of affairs! It was at least a counter-irritant. I didn't notice the labor pains for some time after that, being more concerned as to where the next breath was coming from. Just as a matter of medical record, I subsequently broke out in a truly classical case of hives, beside which even Frank's rashes and swellings seemed mild.

At this point I was wheeled into the operating room, a gleaming white marble place where, it suddenly dawned on me, the cold must be terrific. Under the greenish light above the table I surveyed my companions. Though I myself was in a fine sweat and clothed only in pajama top, they were all bundled to the ears. The English-speaking nurse had a dark blue sweater showing through her white uniform. The white-garbed nun who stood at my head had an extra cape over her shoulders. The young army medic was correctly robed and gloved, but he seemed to have a retinue of young medical corpsmen who had probably come along to see the sights as much as to assist, and each of them was wearing an army field jacket.

This odd sartorial touch seemed to epitomize the circumstances surrounding the advent of the little mite of humanity who was soon dangling protesting from the doctor's big gloved hand.

"She has awfully big feet," the doctor remarked cheerfully. But the fact was she was an awfully thin baby and her feet looked abnormally large on her pencil-thin legs. The Italian diet and I had waged a constant feud in the months preceding her birth, and the only milk available had been half a liter a day from the work oxen of the neighboring farm. If she had lacked proper nourishment, she had been deprived as well of the peace and tranquility so highly regarded by the medical profession as the proper prenatal atmosphere. Adding together the excursions and alarums of the past nine months, plus the turmoil and anxieties awaiting us in the months following her homecoming when she no doubt existed on highly adrenaline-spiked milk, it seemed likely that she would be endowed either with leonine courage or mouse-like timidity.

As a matter of fact, her commonest phrase after she learned to talk turned out to be, "What was dat noise?" accompanied by a transfixed expression in her beaver-brown eyes.

She is six years old now and no one has ever been able to induce her to talk on the telephone. She is learning to read, write, and figure in a French school and her report card invariably carries the following comment:

"*Excellent resultats. Il est dommage qu' Elisabetta soit si timide.*" (Exellent results. It is a pity that Elisabeth is so timid.)

15

Life Can Be Beautiful—Temporarily

I thought I had prepared a cunning nest. I had lain awake nights plotting out all the angles. A baby needs a warmish atmosphere, but not one bedroom in the villa was heated. It occurred to me, at last, that the hitherto closed-off "guest room" was just back of the wall of the living room where the big fireplace was located, hence the flue must pass up the common wall.

Sure enough, when I investigated, I found a rough spot under the wallpaper which testified to the fact that a stovepipe hole had once been there. That was the first requisite taken care of. The Italians make a clever heating stove of terra cotta. Its firebox is made of fire brick and is surmounted by hollow tiles through which the heat circulates, warming the thick tile. You can lay your hand on the surface of the stove at almost any point and not be burned, but the slow, steady heat is being radiated into the room and it remains warm long after the fire has gone out. One of these Becchi stoves would be ideal for this little room.

Since babies and washing seem to be almost synonymous—washing of hands, of diapers, of little pink bottoms among other things—water was the next essential. And this room, by some miraculous coincidence, had a washbowl with hot and cold running water.

I looked around the small room, which had French doors opening onto a tiny, rickety balcony, and I furnished it in my mind as a nursery. True, the room was oddly placed in the house. You turned off from the stair landing across from the upstairs salon, and you entered a little *anticamera*, one step up from the landing. Across the *anticamera* you stepped down one step into the guest room. Overhead was the attic area which had once housed chickens and now was a rats' rendezvous where a very lively business went on by night. Still, identifiable noises were tolerable, I reasoned. The noises hard to bear were the thuds and creaks in remote parts of the house where you couldn't be sure it was anything so minor as a foraging rat.

I broke the news to Frank that I had decided upon the guest room as a nursery. He looked at me commiseratingly and reminded me that it had always been considered the least desirable room in the house.

"It has heat and running water," I pointed out—and added hastily, in order to stem the flow of uncomplimentary remarks about the state of my judgment I saw coming on—"that is, it *will* have as soon as you buy a Becchi stove and get someone to unclog the drain."

But it was too small. Where would you put a stove and still get a bed in the place?

A small stove, I said, and a crib. Not the two bulky single beds with hay-filled mattresses made up as a *matrimoniale* which now took up most of the room.

There would, I calculated, also be room for a cot for me, and the little slipper chair, and some marble-topped antique that could be converted into a bath and diaper-changing table.

Frank sighed, anticipating the usual furniture shifting, but he knew he was defeated and acquiesced.

And so it was finally ready. The long, long, dotted-Swiss curtains over the French doors were washed and ironed, not without considerable travail and anguish on the part of Maria who, in the midst of ironing them, suddenly decided she wasn't equal to such a delicate task and we had had to send them out to a laundry to be finished at a cost of about six dollars and not a little loss of respect on the part of Maria who, I realized too late, had really expected me to order her to finish them regardless.

I had robbed the rest of the house of appropriate rugs and chairs, so that finally the little bedroom was sweet, warm, and immaculate, and the *anticamera* was a cozy little sitting room whose one big window looked out, above the tops of the hedges which shut off the view from the lower floor, toward the lovely mountains east of Rome.

So it was to this room that we brought the minute Pebble. One minor tragedy marked the homecoming—there was not only no hot water, but no water at all from the faucets of the little lavatory, nor in the bathroom which was just through the wall from the baby's room but had to be reached circuitously via the salon. Elettra, it appeared, in "attending to everything" had forgotten to divert the water so that it passed through the pump and had consequently burned out the motor that pumped water to the second floor, an error she paid for in extra work for she had then to carry water to supply the upstairs needs.

But the little stove exuded its gentle heat. Elettra and her daughter had gathered the last flowers from the garden and placed them, together with the plumy heads of pampas grass and various other kinds of seed-pods, here and there about the salon in arrangements that would have done justice to the ladies of a suburban garden club.

How I loved the villa on that day of homecoming! As an old hand at hospitals, I have always found that home, after a session in those aseptic precincts, takes on a radiance that more than compensates for all clinical adversities. Beauty and warmth and coziness are multiplied in proportion to the severity of the recent ordeal. Old paint looks new. Faded colors glow as if retouched for the occasion. The common smells of herbs and cooking food, of ironings, of garden flowers and furniture polish and wood smoke are incense on the air.

Elettra brought me wonderful broth with homemade noodles and even a dish of some kind of tiny dumplings with an onion sauce revered in the Abbruzzi mountains as a milk-stimulant, which, to my considerable surprise, it proved to be.

Things were placid and wonderful for the time being. Our breakfasts were served at a little table by the window in the *anticamera*. Dinners were served across the hall in the big salon before the fire. Frank was working nights in Rome and returned home about two o'clock in the morning, a time which coincided nicely with the baby's feeding, so we brewed tea on a little electric plate and had a cozy snack at that odd hour while Frank briefed me on the state of the world and I briefed him on the domestic front.

This idyllic setup was to be short-lived, however. There came a time when I decided I had to go downstairs to check up on things in general. Probably if I had never gone downstairs that winter we would have gone on in blissful ignorance of Elettra's shortcomings. The thing that aroused my suspicions was that the drinking glasses had a more and more murky appearance and I decided I must re-educate Elettra about dishwashing.

When I went into the kitchen, the sight that met my eyes was enough to shake my faith in Elettra to the depths. The kitchen was long uncleaned. Dirty dishes were stacked everywhere. My red-trimmed white curtains, so painstakingly made and hung, were twisted into grimy loops and tied up out of the way. And Elettra was asking for her usual afternoon off.

I bounced back from the proverbial ceiling and asked her how she could *think* of having the afternoon off with all this work still undone. She looked injured. "But *Signora mia*," she said in her most wheedling tone, "I have *every* afternoon off."

In vain I tried to make it clear to her that she would certainly not have had every afternoon off if I had known how much work she was leaving undone.

"But I have an urgent appointment," she said. "I must go now but I will be back early."

Urgente appointments are so common among Italian help that I knew it was useless to argue. The homeless, the jobless, the indigent in Italy have more *urgente* business than the President of the Republic.

Standing in the appalling mess of the kitchen while Elettra went off on her urgent affairs, I realized that I had brought this "afternoon off" theory upon myself. Before I took her on full time I had tried her out with hour work in the mornings. Her wages for this hourly employment came to about the same, in hard lire, as what we gave her after she theoretically "lived in," but when she lived in she had a room plus full board for herself and her fourteen-year-old daughter. The difference to us was considerable in outlay of food, not to mention clothing we had supplied the two. But of course Elettra reasoned that if she could have done the work in four hours previously, she could just go on working four or five hours a day and then take her usual afternoon off.

At the moment I was not able to take on the household myself, and there was nothing to do but to tolerate Elettra for a while longer. But as the weeks passed it was gradually borne in upon us that Elettra was possessed of an impenetrable stupidity and a total irresponsibility. I was deeply disappointed. I had taken an immediate shine to Elettra. She had a striking gypsy face, great doe-like eyes, and that impelling, husky voice. Her daughter was a pretty, quiet girl. I had thought (with my faultless instinct for misjudging character) that here were two people we would like to have permanently in our household. We had even talked of letting her take the younger "backward" child out of the *collegio* to live with us as well. Fortunately the episode of the dirty tumblers occurred before we had them all installed under our roof.

Elettra, as I was to discover, had a splendid indifference to the value of property. When our lights went out, as they did frequently,

Elettra in the kitchen had placed her candles in two antique cut-glass candlesticks which she had taken from the dining room. "Why did you take these?" I demanded, when I discovered them perched perilously behind the gas plate.

"But *Signora*," she said, regarding me with her great sad eyes, "I had to have *something* to put the candles in." I sent her to the garbage pile to get a couple of empty beer bottles for the candles.

Though the room she insisted upon retaining in a house in the village was unheated, and probably in all her Abbruzzi mountain days she had lived in unheated houses except for the warmth generated by the donkey and the cow, still Elettra was unhappy with her unheated quarters in the villa.

"Elettra," I said, "*we* only have heat on account of the baby, and if you would bestir yourself and move faster and get the work done you wouldn't be so cold."

Still, I let her come with a brazier and get coals from the fire in the Becchi stove to set in her bedroom to take the chill off. She would heap the coals into her fire bucket—a clay pot with a handle specifically designed for the purpose—and would stand in the center of the rug swinging it casually while she regaled me with some unimportant narrative. In the entrance hall below were two quite good large rugs and I knew she had to cross these, as well, to get to her room. Every day I held my breath while Elettra blithely swung her fire about between my room and her own.

Painstakingly I had instructed Elettra in my way of washing diapers. I had soap-flakes for the purpose instead of the crude laundry soap then available in Italy, and these being very precious I always hated to see the fine suds thrown out, especially since the diapers had been previously rinsed and boiled. It was my idea of economy that rugs and dust-cloths and other such articles could be washed in the remaining suds. This economy I tried to convey to Elettra. How well I succeeded I discovered the following morning when I found her washing the tea towels in the diaper suds.

"Elettra," I cried, horrified, "*not* the dishtowels!"

"But *Signora*," she said, in her most injured tone, "you *said* I was to use the water for other things."

Elettra's defections were never malicious. They were simply the outgrowth of her easygoing character and the simplicity of her background. If you had grown up in a dirt-floored hovel in an Italian mountain village, how could you be expected to know that antique glass candlesticks were of any more value than an empty beer bottle—they served the same purpose, didn't they? If you had never gone beyond the third grade in school, how could you be expected to be impressed by scientific views on the nature of disease? If you had never had hot water, or much of any water at all except what you carried on your head from the village fountain, naturally you wouldn't waste it washing dishes. If you had never had a key to your door or any property another might covet, naturally you would be indifferent to the importance of locking up someone else's house at night.

This failure to lock up the house at night was a serious point, and I tried to impress Elettra by telling her of the various break-ins we had experienced ourselves or known of in the neighborhood. I told her, also, that I kept a gun handy in case of emergency. Elettra was evidently impressed at last. She said good night and went on downstairs assuring me that she would forthwith bolt the kitchen door. A little while later she came back and stood in the doorway.

"*Signora*," she said in her slow, mellow voice, "I was just wondering…is there a bell downstairs somewhere that *we* could ring to call *you* in case we are afraid in the night?"

It was a contingency the designers of Italian houses—and indeed of Italian society—had not prepared for. The bell system operated entirely in the opposite direction. The *Signori* could ring for the help but not even in the direst emergency could the help ring for the *Signori*.

The locking of doors and the necessity for it, which Elettra now belatedly acknowledged, evidently served to arouse her previously unawakened sense of peril. Whereas she had claimed at first to be entirely fearless, even to the extent of sleeping with the door unlocked, she now became reluctant to spend the nights in the villa, and begged to be permitted to go home to her own room at night. Her utility to me was obviously narrowing, but still it was just before Christmas and I had all the usual pre-Christmas details to attend to plus the care of the new baby. I agreed to let her go home at night, which left Marta and the baby and me the only occupants of the house when Frank was at work in Rome. We would try to carry on this way until after the holidays and then make some other arrangement.

There were not many days left, so one fine morning I planned my Christmas shopping trip into the city, my first excursion away from the villa since the baby's arrival. With my list in my hand I called

Elettra and prepared to outline to her the things she would need to do for the baby in my absence.

"But *Signora*," she protested, "I am going out today. I am going to visit my child at the *collegio*."

I am sure that at that moment Bandini's previous description of me as "*nervosa*" could have been aptly applied. I was well aware that Elettra had never had that hard schooling as a domestic which, in an Italian home, would have permitted her one stipulated half day off a week, but it seemed to me that ordinary common sense would have made it obvious to her that her own plans had to be subordinated to the plans of her employers—at least occasionally.

The rage into which I flew would have done justice to Maria herself, and out of the smoke and debris of the explosion I think it became abundantly clear to Elettra that either she change her plans or she didn't need to bother coming back after her excursion to the *collegio*.

Elettra's plans, unlike my own, however, were always unchangeable. *I* stayed at home.

16

Merry Roman Christmas

Saint Nicholas—patron saint of children, marriageable girls, students, mariners, merchants, and thieves—who, in the guise of a plump old gentleman with a white beard and a red suit has managed to establish himself in a position of considerable prominence in the American Christmas tradition, finds himself in Italy running a poor second to an unprepossessing female character known as the Befana.

The Befana, or good witch, doesn't get around to Italian homes on December 25th, but appears instead at Epiphany. Nonetheless, with her hooked nose, her bag of gifts, and her broomstick, she gets top billing all through the Christmas season in the land where Saint Nicholas's bones lie buried and where his charges, the merchants, have succeeded in building the old idea of gifts for the infant Jesus up into almost as fantastic and profitable a commercial enterprise as we know it in America.

There is also in Italy a character known as Father Christmas—Babbo Natale—who is an undernourished version of our conception of Santa Claus. Tall and thin instead of short and stout, his red coat is ankle length and flaps about his legs a bit disconsolately, for he is usually depicted as striding off in a great hurry, tradition having failed to provide him with a means of conveyance for his rounds. Whether Babbo Natale and Saint Nicholas are the same is a moot point. It is certain, however, that the Befana is a more reliable and more widely acclaimed bringer of gifts to the good and meter-out of lumps of coal to the naughty.

All of these diverse conceptions naturally complicated our first Italian Christmas. Though Marta at six had already had her Christmas personnel established on a non-material basis, still it was a bit confusing to reconcile the kindly old Santa she had always visualized with his thinner half-brother who is dominated by a female specter straight out of our Halloween tradition.

The only way you could compromise between Christmas-and-Santa on the 25th of December, and the Befana with her bag of gifts on January 6th was, of course, to give the nod to both. In addition there was the marvelous innovation of the *presepio*, or Christmas manger scene. Not that the crib is unknown to American children, but in Italy it is on a much grander scale. Though our traditional tree is often absent from Italian homes, even the humblest manage to gather together the makings of a *presepio*. Figures in various sizes can be bought in any little *merceria* in the holiday season, but the real place to buy them is in Piazza Navona in the heart of old Rome, where each year is held a veritable fair for candy, toys, gifts and figurines. Here are booth after booth of clay angels, wise men, lambs, shepherds, Holy Families, donkeys, palms, and stars. Gaily painted and touched with gilt, they can be had in simple terra cotta or in another substance guaranteed *infrangibile* which does indeed stand a few more knocks than the clay.

Thus we were met with another compromising situation which could be solved with the least agony simply by bowing to both traditions. We must have a tree and a *presepio*. From this it is readily seen that Christmas for an American child in Italy rises to new heights of glamour. It has the further advantage, too, that it lasts over a period of months until the meticulous postal system which opens, inspects, and then rewraps and seals all parcels, has delivered the last of the packages from friends and relatives in America who are, of course, extra generous to the poor little American child so far away from home and the "advantages" thereof.

In 1946 the American population of Rome, aside from the remaining military, was still not so numerous as to put a premium on Christmas trees. We found a lovely tree on the Spanish Steps, a market place we later learned to avoid as being too central and hence more costly. Jeeped home to the villa, the tree was set up in the studio before the big windows, and the decorations we had thoughtfully brought with us to a country which turns them out like popcorn in fantastic array, were put in place. Under it we set our modest *presepio*.

Christmas came with its gifts, and in due time the Befana also arrived. From then on until Easter, occasional Christmas boxes came in the mail. It was a truly Roman festival but in spite of all the obvious advantages, our insatiable young still complained that it was not up to an American Christmas. The thing lacking, of course, was the snow, which Rome rarely provides for the holiday trade and in search of which many people spend the season in the mountain villages, where can even be found a living *presepio* with villagers acting out the nativity scene.

By the time another Christmas came around, everything had changed at the villa. The Bandinis, whose daughter Rita had initiated Marta into the ways of the Befana by placing their shoes side by side on the hearth on the eve of Epiphany, were no longer there. Lina was involved with the settling of her new apartment in the city. Elettra's departure had occurred the week before Christmas. My shopping expedition never came off. All the frenzied last-minute things that usually seem so inevitably a part of Christmas just never were done at all, and strangely enough, it didn't seem to make any difference. Last year's *presepio* was brought out of its wrappings, the tree ornaments were refurbished and were more than adequate for the little tree we set up in a corner of the *anticamera* where it was warm and cozy. Boxes arrived from America. A gift or two got purchased in a casual and incidental manner. And, all in all, it was one of our more memorable Christmases.

A subtle change had come over the atmosphere in the House of the Four Winds from the day Elettra departed. We were alone at last. Like many people with little or no voice, I often feel like singing, a luxury which I deny myself when any outsider, even a maid, is around to hear. I am not averse to inflicting my inharmonies on the hapless members of my family, however, so when I felt like singing I sang. When I felt like running around the house in my scanties, I ran around the house in my scanties. I didn't have to be *"la Signora"* any longer. Frank shed *"il Signore"* likewise with a feeling of relief. For the first time in two years—for the first time, really, in seven years considering those absent five—we were united as a family with no intrusions or complications, no giving of orders or receiving of complaints. No arguments—what luxury!

As for the work, well, the beautiful laundress was pleased to come back again. The cleaning woman came once a week, as always. The rest we did ourselves and we discovered that our dependence upon "help" for the various little chores around the house had been largely a state of mind. As a matter of fact we reaped some unexpected benefits from our servantless state, for about this time occurred what we like to refer to as the miracle of the water, but what actually was the logical result of some simple efficiency methods.

As long as the running of the house had been in the hands of hired help, we hadn't bothered much about certain obvious malpractices which could always be justified by some elaborate and invincible reasoning, and by the subtle underlying suggestion that the

Signori shouldn't bother their pretty heads about any practical matters. But the constant wastage of water all over the premises was something that bothered us, in view of the sometimes total absence of water in large sections of the city. Here in the villa we had streams running off constantly in various directions. One flowed into the irrigation tanks whenever there was an excess from house use. This made sense in summer when it was eventually used to water the garden, but it flowed as well during the winter and dribbled off over the hill into the neighbor's fields. Another stream flowed constantly from an open faucet in the laundry where it kept a huge cement vat filled and then it, too, overflowed making a permanently soggy strip through the peasant's fields where the weeds grew rank and the grain died out.

Turn this water off? The Bandinis had been ready with twenty-five kinds of reasons why it had to flow continuously, which all added up to the one reason, "Here in Italy we like *running* water." If water were not *corrente*, it seemed, it was unpalatable, unhealthful, warm, and dangerous. It appeared it would have been as sensible on our part to have suggested turning off the wind or the sunshine. Nevertheless, after the departure of the Bandinis and Elettra we hazarded the foolhardy risk of going against nature and tradition, and we turned off the water though we had to get a new faucet to do it, the old one having been permanently affixed in the open position by years of disuse. We closed, as well, the faucet to the irrigation tanks for the winter season.

Frank, in his daily attention to the electric motor which pumped water to the upstairs tanks, began to have ever more lurid ideas of transgressing the ancient system. Peering among the network of pipes which led to and from the motor like veins and arteries from a heart, it suddenly occurred to him that the water was flowing in some circuitous manner whereas it could just as well be connected more directly. Summoning a plumber, he said, "Connect *this* pipe with *that* pipe," and this the workman proceeded to do, with a pitying glance at the Americans with streamlined notions.

"It is the same thing in the end," the workman said, "whether the water runs through this new piece of pipe or through the old ones." The difference, to Frank's incisive engineering brain, was that now the water always ran via the motor so that you couldn't make the disastrous mistake of forgetting to turn it through when the motor was on, hence no more burning out of the motor. Even Frank, genius that he was, was not prepared however for the further advantages accruing from this piece of strategy.

I was passing through the salon the following afternoon when I heard the drip, drip of water on the tiles outside the window. This, when the motor was running, was the sign that the attic tanks were full and overflowing. But the motor was not on, and had not been on since the day before. Frank was not even at home at the moment so he could not be down there fiddling with the motor. Unless some unknown hand had turned the switch, the motor should be off and the tanks should be almost empty pending their being refilled that night.

With a slight tingling in the region of the vestigial hackles, I went down to the basement to check on the motor. It was not on. Then I plodded all the way back up to the attic and took a look into the tanks which were, unmistakably, full and overflowing onto the roof! Undoubtedly a miracle. I rushed to the phone to tell Frank the glad news.

For nearly two years we had been fighting the losing fight of the motor. First stolen, then twice burned out, we had been without water for long periods on each occasion. Now, by the simple process of turning off the faucets where water had been wasting, and by making a direct connection in the pipes, we had a gravity system that worked splendidly with no help from a motor!

Whenever we solved, either by accident or intuition, one of the innumerable problems of the house, we enjoyed a period of cocky satisfaction which compensated us for many of the travails. Just now, on this second Christmas, we were on the crest of an egotistical wave over our success with the water—what if we did have chores to do and no one to lay out our pajamas at night, we were having fun.

We ate our Christmas dinner at the little table in front of the fireplace upstairs. The wintry sun fell through the south windows in shafts of blue above the dull red tiles of the floor. The fire crackled companionably. We had neither guests nor servants, but a new sense of completeness, for this Christmas, instead of three, we were four.

When the dinner was all ready, it suddenly occurred to me that I had forgotten to get any wine, a scandalous omission in Italy. "Oh," I said apologetically, "I've forgotten the wine!"

Frank rose and majestically swept up our glasses.

"Wine, indeed!" he said. "We have water, haven't we?" And he marched off to fill our goblets from the bathroom tap.

"This," he said, returning, "is on the house."

17

"How Silently, How Silently..."

A little gray-haired lady with hands clasped behind her back stood at the foot of the crib and looked down into the sleeping face of the new baby, across whose doll-like features played the ghost of a smile, like the flicker of sunlight under breeze-stirred boughs.

"They say it's only gas," I said deprecatingly of the smile, not wanting to seem to believe, as of course I did, that my baby was exceptional.

"Oh, well!" she said in a spirited voice, tossing her head, as if to imply that *they* were cynics and why shouldn't there be little fleeting dreams of joy passing through the fresh, untrammeled brain. And then, in a different voice, almost as if she were talking to herself, a soft yet resonant voice, each word precise and mellow as a jewel:

"How silently, how silently, the wondrous gift is given..." she quoted.

It was somehow such a surprising and a right thing to say. I thought of the various comments I had heard people make at the crib-side of a new baby, struggling to say something complimentary and kind, and ending with something lame and inexact like, "How cute!" over the mite of humanity still bearing birth bruises and a preview of senility in its minute features.

But this was different. Here was a comment that struck deeper than appearances. "How silently, how silently, the wondrous gift is given..." It spoke of the mystery at the core of being. It implied a benediction upon the small dreaming object as well as the beholder. It hinted comfortably of an indwelling spirit of continuity and divinity.

For a moment, there in the room, in the stillness, while the clock ticked and the fire whispered in the flue and the words and the sound of her voice seemed to hang suspended in time like a tangible fusion of several of the nobler aspects of the human soul—for a moment the room became the cave on the outskirts of Bethlehem. The Magi converged. The cynics of scientific analysis went limping out the door. Gas indeed!

It was my first real acquaintance with Miss Thomas, the English lady whom I had phoned to ask if she could come to tutor Marta since our means of getting her to a regular school had failed. I did not know then, as I came to know later, that the essence and the substance of her character and her spirit were in that quotation, that to Emma Thomas the star bends low for any newborn babe, no matter how humble. In each of her fellowmen she sees the spark of divine fire and regards it as worth fanning and sustaining, and by virtue of sheer personal kindliness wherever she has gone in her long and busy life she has been dispersing the forces of cynicism and fortifying the ramparts of faith in humankind.

It was under other skies than the bright, metallic blue of Italy's that Emma Thomas was born and first became aware of the wonders of the world around her. She was the daughter of London shopkeepers who, judging by her well-remembered anecdotes, must have been persons of rare good humor and spirit. "Come for a walk, Emmy?" her boot-maker father used to say, and they would set off without any objective, exploring the country byways, eating when they came upon an inn, returning by whatever conveyance was available when they were tired. Once, she recalls, they walked for eleven miles before they came to a place for refreshment!

Those walks were excellent training for the sturdy pair of legs that still, at eighty, carried her briskly about the streets of Rome, trotting past the Romans who proceed at what she calls the "Roman crawl." They were excellent training for the eyes that still read without glasses and observed, as then, the minute beauties of the natural world, the moods of weather, the changes of season.

They were excellent training for the memory that still, at eighty, reached back to her second year—and never failed in the lists of lessons, appointments, meetings that crowded her Roman days, for it was on those walks as well as at other times that her father played his game of mental arithmetic. "Eleven, add seven, take away five, times two—got it?"

She went on, then, in the gray and smoky atmosphere of the great city which was not without its special beauty, amidst the busy confusion of family birthings and illnesses and deaths, to become a practiced hand with the younger ones, a wiper of noses and a teller of stories. She was only thirteen when she became a student teacher under the British system of teacher apprenticeship. Then came Stockwell Training College, and finally the new and exciting London School of Economics in the days of the Webbs and other famous Fabians. Here she was the first woman ever to take an honors degree in Sociology.

As we came to appreciate later, Miss Thomas is that rare thing, a born and inspired teacher. For over sixty–seven of her eighty years she had been teaching continuously in various parts of the globe, under diverse circumstances, with or without "equipment," with or without a salary. Her contacts and associations reached from Jane Addams to Mahatma Gandhi—and back to the Italian gatekeeper's children with equal interest and pride.

But all these things I did not know that day when she came to see about lessons for Marta. I had only sensed, seeing her for a brief time as directress of studies of the English language school in Rome, that here was a distinguished and gentle lady whose English put to shame my own sloppy "American." Had I known then the excellence of her training and experience I would have hesitated to call her to teach the three R's to a seven-year-old, but I didn't know, and she was without the false professional pride that would have prevented many a graduate of an institution such as the London School of Economics from stooping so low in the pedagogical field. To her, as I was to find out, teaching is teaching, and vistas of a more tolerant, more kindly, more abundant spiritual life can be opened even in—or especially in— the mere beginner's mind.

It was Miss Thomas who broke the spell. "You know," she said brightly, "I am very good with babies. I was the eldest of seven, so I've had a great deal of experience."

We discussed then the details of her coming out to the villa to give lessons to Marta, and she undertook the work, for after considerable urging she named a ridiculously low fee. She would come three afternoons a week and she was completely undaunted by the fact that she would have to ride the six or eight kilometers up from Rome in the miserable, dirty little tramcars, crowded in among the country people and their market baskets.

We went out into the courtyard to find Marta and apprise her of the arrangement. Then Miss Thomas took her departure. Her handclasp made me wince and left indentations from my ring, and dispelled any misapprehension I may have had as to the fragility of this person, who only in point of years could be said to be old.

And so for Marta—who had already sampled American kindergarten, an English language school in Rome in its larval stage, an Italian private Catholic school, a bit of tutoring by the Italian *Signorina*, and a smattering of my own attempt at teaching—there began a new type of education which made all the alleged benefits of classroom training (except possibly the association with other children) tame by comparison.

Under the mulberry trees, across the courtyard, down the *viale*, out into the garden among the cabbages they played follow-the-leader,

the brisk figure of Miss Thomas, hands clasped behind her back in characteristic stance, and the long-legged child in shorts, one behind the other, singing French *chansons* as they went, pausing to study a praying mantis on a twig, picking up a bright pebble and learning something of the story of geology. Never, I thought, had pleasure and learning been so harmoniously combined.

There were sessions, of course, of more formal study when they sat together at a table, Marta sketching interminably while Miss Thomas explained some problem or related an anecdote out of her rich memories to point up some theory. They played the game of mental arithmetic. Sometimes Marta would be lying flat on her back on the rug during these sessions, and my sense of propriety was shocked, but Miss Thomas waved aside my anxiety. "I never mind," she said, "if pupils get into comfortable positions, so long as they are interested." Still, it seemed to me that a certain disrespect for the teacher was implied in this casual attitude. Miss Thomas thought not. She was an old hand at liberal ideas in education. Long before progressivism became a theory—and an issue—in American education, she had been working toward liberalizing the pupil-teacher relationship. "Greater freedom for the child and greater trust in the child's personality," as she expressed it. But freedom itself she regarded as a kind of discipline. "You are not free in the water," she sagely pointed out, "until you have learned to swim," leaving me to reflect upon the conclusion that, as she phrased it, freedom is capacity.

When Miss Thomas had finished her thirty years of teaching in the London school system, she "retired" at 51 to implement her dream of a better way of educating children. She opened a school in Switzerland. Known as the Fellowship School, in those years between the wars this school became a little island of brotherhood in a sea of national tensions. Children of all nationalities were welcome and their differences soon vanished in an atmosphere of mutual trust and respect. Except for a cook there was no domestic staff and all the work was done by the teachers and the children themselves.

"We felt," Miss Thomas explained, "that if children were not dictated to, they would tend to turn naturally to their elders for help and advice." An effort was made to eliminate as far as possible the barriers between teachers and students, with the result that all— teachers and students alike—were interested in learning. So there in the Fellowship School for nearly fifteen years the principles of cooperative democracy were not only taught to but lived by children from all parts of the world.

These facts regarding Miss Thomas's theories and background came out one by one during our conversations before and after the lesson hours. It is a question whether Marta or I benefited the most from those three afternoons a week. Marta absorbed information like a sponge, while I had someone with whom to discuss theories of education, baby care, personality problems, religion—and household crises.

If we were without help, Miss Thomas pitched in and washed the dishes or carried wood for the fires. A Quaker for many years, she had been long schooled in the philosophy which puts friendship and usefulness to others ahead of personal ambition and false pride. She makes friends and finds ways of being useful wherever she goes.

There were the years of the siege of London when she served as a fire warden; the later years of the war when singlehanded she cared for fifteen evacuee children in a country house in England. She had helped on English farms during World War I, and one of her proudest accomplishments was her ability to milk a cow. There was a brief visit in Chicago when she took on a class of Mexicans preparing for citizenship, teaching them English though she knew not a word of Spanish. She taught English to Italian prisoners of war in England, and when she came to Rome after the war she taught English to dozens of Italians, with or without compensation according to their means. She tutored many a laggard schoolchild with his Latin or his math. She trotted all over Rome, knocking on the doors of ministers or judges, to try to find living quarters or justice for some poor Italian about to be evicted. She was a one-woman distribution agency for clothes and kindnesses to poverty-ridden Italians.

In a situation where Emma Thomas cannot be useful she has little desire to remain. It was for this reason that she finally "retired" from her work in Rome and went to Perugia where a wider field seemed to be opening. She felt that, with the resumption of regular schools, the increase of available tutors, the better staffing of relief agencies and the Quaker center, her work in Rome was no longer as vital as it had been—even though her pupils still included, among others, a high official of the Italian government who had come to lean upon her not only as a teacher of English but as a friend and confidante as well.

Long an advocate of nonviolence, Miss Thomas found in the ancient but liberal city of Perugia a little nucleus of workers for a better and more peaceful world. Undaunted by the rumors of war rumbling ominously about the globe, they work busily and enthusiastically (much in the spirit of the saint of Assisi whose feet once trod those very hills and vales, and of Gandhi) to implement their dream of a kinder, more humane civilization.

There is a steady trickle of idealists through the world from end to end who steer steadfastly by some fixed star of hope and charity and brotherhood, and they coalesce from time to time into a thin stream that flows toward some pool of mutual faith and work. Perugia is such a pool, and chief among its wellsprings is the mind and spirit of the little, plainly-dressed, gray-haired lady who taught French to a leggy seven-year-old by singing French songs under the ilex trees; who stood one day at the foot of a crib in a room that looks out on the Sabine hills, and finished the quotation for an ignorant and absent-minded mother...

"So God imparts to human hearts the blessings of His heaven."

18

By the Dawn's Early Light

At the risk of being forever shunned by my friends of the cocktail circuit whose eyes come reluctantly unglued only after eleven a.m., I am about to make a shameful confession which up to now I have tried to conceal from all except the immediate family—I *like* getting up early in the morning.

There it is, and I suppose I'm finished socially, so I might as well admit further that I like doing all the homely old chores such as cooking and cleaning cupboards and polishing silverware. I'm sure the Count suspected all this, and my honorably calloused palms gained me no grace in the eyes of the Bandinis, but quite a few years of getting up and stirring around and, as Lina used to say, "doing and making," have left their ineffaceable mark on my character as well.

As a matter of fact I was corrupted quite early in youth by having been assigned the task of "bringing in the horses," which involved getting up in the cold mountain dawn, saddling the pony, and dashing off across the sparkling pasture scattering meadowlarks, splashing through the mint-bordered creek, and hunting among the willows for the work horses which, when they saw me, sighed resignedly and headed for the barn, snatching a last good, bitter mouthful of willow as they went.

When an impressionable child of nine is given a start like that, what can you expect? Exactly—the subsequent ninety years of nostalgia for oblique shadows falling westward, the soft plop of hooves in dew-laid dust, the smell of crushed mint not necessarily surrounded by a frosted glass.

So there at the villa after the turn of the year when we were getting along without help, I had quite a refreshing experience for a few weeks. My days began at dawn when Felix, the poodle, walked me down the *viale*. Not that *he* cared so much about getting out early. By choice he was very continental in his habits. But I had certain functions to perform relative to the baby, and once on my feet at six it seemed silly to go back to bed, so Felix condescended to show me around outside. He had certain favorite clumps of grass to visit. He had to give the cats a modicum of discipline, and he took his constitutional by chasing stones thrown down the *viale*.

The morning air was fresh and invigorating, but he was much too French to permit himself to give the impression of enjoying anything so simple, so I don't know just how far Felix shared my enthusiasm for these sprightly beginnings of the day, but as for me I seemed to tap a well of energy that sent me sailing through my chores not only with enthusiasm but with pleasure.

Breakfasts—what had they been these two years? *Caffe-latte*, yesterday's rolls warmed over (since we were not near enough to a bakery to have them fresh). Now, once more, the splendid aroma of bacon and eggs filled the kitchen. Pancakes, hot muffins, baking-powder biscuits piping hot and dripping honey! And no having it brought to us on a tray in the *anticamera*. "Breakfast's ready!" shouted up the staircase as in an old farm house, "Break-f-a-s-t!"

The stems of wild iris that had sometimes come along on the tray, I went out now and pulled them myself from under the syringa bushes along the *viale*. I heard the cool, cork-drawing sound as the sheath gave up its ivory-ended stalk. I smelled the earth and the leaf-mold and the drifting wood-smoke from the house of the farmer over the hill. I heard the carts rumbling by on the road to market, the jingling of harness bells, the snapping of whips. I saw the morning light enlarge and change and the westward-reaching shadows shorten in the courtyard.

This is supposed to be adversity, I would reflect gloatingly, being "stuck without a maid," and I would go back into the big morning-bright kitchen with my hands full of blue flags, and the muffins would be just browning in the portable oven and the coffee would be perking. And upstairs my new and lovely baby would be stirring again and when I thought of her my breasts would tingle sharply with the in-rushing of sustenance, and I would walk way up above the tiles in my vanity and joy for all the things I could do and make and experience and provide.

So we put off, from day to day, getting another maid and we enjoyed an interlude of privacy and being-togetherness that more than compensated for the extra work involved.

Still, it had to be a temporary way of life. I met the *contadini* along the hedgerows when I walked the dog, and they looked at me as if I were certainly something escaped from the big institution up the hill. No *Signora* in their experience had ever walked the dog before seven a.m., if indeed she had ever walked the dog at all. Via the village grapevine, they knew all about our servantless state and they could surmise to what other tasks the lady of the house was turning her hand indoors. One thing or the other, they probably concluded: either *la Americana* is no *Signora* at all or else she is quite strange in the head.

They were right on both counts, of course. Up to a certain point doing one's own housework and cooking is zestful and amusing and satisfying. It is also, in the long run, very tiring. In a country where household help is plentiful and inexpensive (and it requires only patience, understanding, and quite a lot of luck to find *good* help), and where household equipment and marketing habits are a century behind the times, it could reasonably be considered a mild form of insanity to continue doing it singlehanded week after week.

The novelty had worn off and the drudgery had set in. There came a morning when I pushed back my coffee cup and rested my chin on my hand and thought, "The hell with it all." Felix had very sensibly gone back to his mat for a rest.

All this sentimental twaddle about making your own biscuits and picking your own vegetables—you can do *that* when you get back to America, I reminded myself. The great panorama that lay just down over the hill began to unfold itself in my mind. I saw the domes and the fountains and the arches—all Rome at my feet and I sitting here thinking I ought to be getting at the dishes!

Better get down into town and explore those interesting old ruins before you become one, I told myself firmly. I went out and bought a newspaper and spent the rest of the morning decoding the situations wanted columns.

19

There's Just One Thing...

We begin in a sensible and systematic manner the process of looking for help. The first step is to alert all one's friends and acquaintances to the fact that you are seeking one of the following:

1) a paragon who is honest, reliable, intelligent, courageous, a good cook—and willing to do everything except, possibly, the family washing

2) two paragons, preferably husband and wife, who have all the above qualities and are willing to do *everything*.

Your friends are solicitous, but vague. Naturally if they knew of any such persons they would employ them themselves on the spot. Somebody knows a maid who is *almost* all that is to be desired, but she wouldn't consider working in the country. Someone else knows of a wonderful maid, but she has a habit of padding the grocery bills and is insulted if it is called to her attention. And then there is that terrific Sardinian couple—but their friends and relatives are always coming to stay with them.

You consult the agencies. They always have long lists of applicants, almost invariably from "*Alt Italia*," which is presumed to mean that they are superior to those from the south. But somehow the agencies' prospects almost always fail to show up. The agency phones repeatedly to inquire whether so and so has kept her appointment. No, she has not come.

From time to time a person seeking work actually arrives at the house and goes into a state of nervous collapse upon being shown the size of the place. Or it turns out to be someone looking for that plum, a *portiere*'s job, which includes living quarters for a sizable brood of children and relatives.

Among those who came was a fine-looking middle-aged woman, clean, quick-moving, willing and able. She had a husband who, according to her description of him, was a man of "presence." He was, she asserted, very intelligent, clean, handsome.

"Very good," we said, "then he can help you with the heavy work and see to locking up the house at night."

The woman sighed. "There's just one thing about my husband," she said, and we prepared ourselves for the description of some minor defect.

"He doesn't work," she concluded simply.

"He doesn't work?"

"No, he just doesn't work. He never has worked. He never will work. He has, however, a very distinguished presence," she added hopefully.

She was so forthright and beguiling a person that we were tempted to take them anyway—but then among the things we felt we could live without was a "distinguished presence" in the house, especially one who no doubt consumed a normal amount of viands while declining to labor.

"I'm sorry," I said, "I'm afraid we can't use you."

"I'm sorry, too," she said, sighing. "It's always the same." And she unburdened herself of her problems in a gentle and patient way. "He's my husband," she said, "and I can't do anything about it." She pulled down the neck of her blouse and showed us a series of scars where he had scratched or hit her in a fit of anger. My face must have expressed my horror of such a character. "But *Signora*," she said, "you should just *see* him. He has *such* a distinguished presence!"

The next couple had anything but distinguished presence. They were quite young and were accompanied on the interview by an uncle, a burly *maresciallo di carabinieri*, some acquaintance of Lina's whom she had contacted in her program of helping us to find help. She herself at the moment was on an upswing of fortune and was in the city briefly between trips hither and yon.

Carlo and Rosina were inexperienced but intelligent, according to their uncle the marshal, and they would rapidly learn whatever was required of them. Rosina was already very *brava* as a cook. I essayed to ask Rosina directly a couple of questions about her capacity, but the uncle intervened.

"There's just one thing about Rosina," he explained. "She's very *timida*." Rosina shot him a look that seemed to be something less than gratitude for coming to her rescue. In any event she remained silent throughout the interview, her only response being a quick nod or shake of the head with downcast eyes. The husband, on the other hand, seemed quite eager about the whole thing so I felt that if Rosina were diffident I could convey my thoughts to her through Carlo until she had courage enough to speak for herself.

Lina, being an old hand in the training of domestic help, saw here a virgin field for her endeavors. They had never been "in service" previously. She would start them out right. She had a vested interest in them anyway, since they were relatives of her friend the *maresciallo*. So she agreed to stay a few days and break them in. They arrived next morning with their suitcase, and Lina set Rosina to work and managed to keep Carlo at various tasks until she had to leave for some engagement in town. The moment she left, Carlo abandoned his labors and took the dog for a walk. Most of the rest of the day he walked the dog. As a dog-walker, Carlo was highly successful and satisfactory, even to Felix who thus far had not had a valet to call his own and took to it like the aristocrat he was.

I watched the dog-walking from an upstairs window and declined to intervene. Rosina knew that Carlo's job was to help her with the heavy work, so I was interested to see whether she had the courage to summon him when she needed him. Rosina never called and never came near. Carlo enjoyed cigarette after cigarette and strolled with Felix in the *viale*.

In the late afternoon with Lina back from her errand, she decided Carlo must be taught to serve. Now there's just one thing about *me*. Regardless of what other meals I may eat during the day, or at what hours I may eat them, I have an unvarying hunger pang that assails me at eleven a.m. and at five p.m. with such regularity that I have been known to set my watch by it. I always drink something at these hours. Usually at eleven it is coffee, and usually at five it is tea, hence we say "coffee-time" and "tea-time," though sometimes I drink tea at coffee-time and sometimes I drink coffee at tea-time. In any event, I usually run to the kitchen and get my snack at eleven and five with no fuss or feathers. If there is company, tea is a more elaborate occasion and we sit down and teeter our cups in our laps and munch cookies or sandwiches.

But this time Lina forbade me to come to the kitchen to get my tea. It would ruin her training of Carlo, she said. I must compose myself in the salon upstairs and ring the bell. She would be downstairs and when I rang she would explain to Carlo that very likely the *Signora* was ready for her tea, but that he must go up to the salon, bow slightly, and say, "*Commandi, Signora.*"

I was to say, "The tea, please, Carlo." Whereupon he would bow slightly, withdraw, and come down to fetch the tea which Rosina meanwhile was preparing.

There was a slight delay—the usual interminable period of waiting for something to be done that you could do yourself in one-tenth the time. I tried to wait in a lady-like repose, but I got restless and began doing something else. Matter of fact I was toying with the idea of washing my hair and had the water drawn and was about to duck my head when I thought, "Good heavens! I can't receive my 'tea' properly in this condition."

I heard steps on the stairs and had to scurry like anything to reach the green chair and assume an indolent pose, but there I was with my ankles crossed and my chin delicately supported on my fingertips looking very much like a *contessa*—or so I imagined—when Carlo arrived with the tea.

"Is that all, Madame?" he asked with what I thought was just a little too much solicitude. And that "Madame"—where had he got that? He should have said "*Signora*." He not only bowed as he withdrew, he clicked his heels. Carlo is no fool, I decided, but he knows how to make one of me.

I told Lina I thought we were overdoing the serving angle, but she was insistent. Our dinner was impeccably served under her eagle eye, and Carlo came and went with that slight, ironic smile and the not-quite-click of the heels that made it impossible to say whether he was being terribly polite or slyly supercilious.

How long this play acting might have continued I can't say, for on the morning of the second day Rosina failed to emerge from her room. Carlo reported to Lina that Rosina was not well, and Lina went to investigate. Rosina was in bed in the darkened room and said she had a terrible *mal di testa*. Lina came to me wringing her hands. "What can I do?" she said. "If she is sick she is sick and I can't make her get up."

I suggested that she send Carlo out to do the marketing and we would get along one way or another.

Carlo had no sooner disappeared down the *viale* than Rosina emerged from her room, red-eyed and voluble. All her shyness had fled away. "That brute my husband!" she cried. "He fixed all this up just to get me to come back to him. I was very happy as long as he was unemployed. I could stay home with Mamma and he lived with his uncle. That old faker! He wanted to get rid of Carlo and Carlo wanted to get me back, so they jumped at the chance to take this job. I didn't want any part of it! I won't sleep with him. He beats me up and he keeps me awake all night! I want to go back to Mamma!" She was, as a matter of fact, in a quite ravaged state.

Lina was desolate. She had been making such strides in training Carlo, and Rosina was not a bad cook. I, on the other hand, was almost

glad to have the facts exonerate my intuition, which had caused me to have a slight feeling of revulsion whenever that suave character, Carlo, glided into the room.

"Carlo would have made an *excellent* servant," Lina lamented.

"There's just one thing about that Carlo," I said authoritatively in my flawless hindsight. "He's a complete little stinker."

We felt really sorry for Rosina, and thought seriously of keeping her as a maid and sending Carlo packing. There was, however, the strong probability that anything so advantageous for Rosina would never be permitted by the sadistic Carlo, and he would be hanging around the place badgering her from then on. Between Mamma and the *maresciallo* they would have to work out their destiny.

Our experience with Italian help having been notably unsuccessful, we began to think of all the displaced persons at loose ends around Rome and surmised that just possibly some of them might be glad of a home away from the monotony and discipline of a camp. Miss Thomas knew of a fine, strapping Yugoslav boy, so she sent him to us. For a few days he pruned the hedges industriously, raked the yard, beat the rugs, locked up the house at night. He was a handsome, brawny, blond boy. Lina called him "*caro*" and visited with him and ate with him and came to us appalled at the amount of food he stowed away. "Three eggs at a meal!" she cried. "Two great bowls of spaghetti! And the bread and marmalade—"

Still, he was very agreeable and his English was enchanting. "I have taken the dog out twice or thrice," he would say. His manners were polished and precise. Though he was not exactly an answer to our problem, he was a great help with some of the long-neglected chores and the yard work, and we would have kept him indefinitely, though we realized that displaced persons were always poised—or so they hoped—on the brink of being sent to whatever country they sought to enter. We could expect that one day Vittorio, too, would get his papers in order to go to South America. We were not prepared for it to happen after only five days, however, and were surprised when he announced that he could not work any longer.

"You are going to South America, then?"

"Well—no, not yet," he confessed hesitantly, and then explained. "My father has found out that I am working," he said, "and he forbids it. My father is a doctor and he regards it as shameful that a son of his should do such work."

Bankrupt of everything but pride, the old European had his way. The strong son went back to the camp to await in idleness his transfer to the promised land.

Once the word got about that we would try "DP's", various people were eager to place friends who were needy and homeless. There was another Yugoslav, a nurse, who had appealed to a friend for help. She was young, strong, and capable and she came to interview us. Yes, she could cook and clean and help with the baby. We showed her the room, and she seemed to find everything satisfactory. She returned in the evening to, as we supposed, settle in. Instead, she had a proposition to make to us. She had a friend in camp, a young man, and since it would be lonely for her in the big downstairs, and we could obviously use a man around the place, she proposed bringing him along to share her—responsibilities, shall we say? He was right outside now in case it was agreeable to us. Unfortunately, it was not.

These two experiences had nearly convinced us that displaced persons were hardly the type to share our big house and our problems. Still our friends persisted in finding us "prospects," and one prospect was too urgently wished upon us to be ignored.

"These friends of ours," said our friend, "are living in a *pensione* and spending 80,000 lire a month for the two of them. They are practically destitute. They are youngish and they speak beautiful English. They have been pushed around Europe for years from country to country. Talk to them, at least. It ought to be advantageous for you and for them."

They were, indeed, a charming and interesting couple. We explained our situation. "Italian domestic help has not worked out for us," we said firmly, "and we are interested in trying a cooperative arrangement in which, in exchange for a home and food, you share the work and responsibilities of the house. Someone must walk Marta to school and back daily, for example. The marketing, cooking, and housework we can do on an equal basis." The gentleman thought accompanying the child to school would be an enjoyable chore for him. We toured the house together, a warm intellectual friendship ripening as we went.

Their room was to be Lina's old room, a handsome and well-furnished room on the ground floor, right next to the dining room. It was unheated, but we pointed out that they could always use the dining room as their sitting room in the evening as we would all be upstairs. In effect they would have the entire lower floor for their use and we would have the upstairs. We would share the kitchen and the dining room at mealtimes.

There was just one thing, they pointed out. One or the other of them would have to go into Rome every day to attend to their "affairs." They would have to get their mail, for example. Something began to tell us that while they were interested in saving 80,000 lire a month in board and room, they were not very much interested in investing their own time and energy in the project. What urgent affairs and correspondence could they have that involved daily trips into the city? I myself went into town once a week or so. Still, we agreed to try out the plan, and we said goodbye until the next day when they would move in with us. It would be great getting their feet on the ground again, working in the garden...

In the evening, we received a telephone call from our newfound friends. There was just one thing—it had occurred to them that since the bedroom was unheated, would we mind very much if they moved their bed into the dining room? There was—oh, yes—just one more thing. There was a very—but very—good Italian maid at the *pensione* who would be willing to come along with them for a very small wage.

I bit a small piece out of the telephone stand at this point, masticated it slowly, drew a long breath, and then said as evenly as possible:

"I'm afraid we have not made the situation quite clear. We do not want any more Italian domestic help in the house, as we explained yesterday. Our own bedrooms are unheated, and since we all use the dining room *as a dining room* it would be quite impossible to convert it into a bedroom. It was very pleasant meeting you and perhaps we will meet again some time."

I was in a desperate hurry to close the conversation for fear they would accept their miserable servantless, heatless proposition of the day before without the modifications they were proposing, and agree to come anyway. My clairvoyance, working as usual in reverse, had suddenly revealed to me that anyone capable of making so monstrous a condition would never fit in. I said goodbye with the definite impression that I had just shoved a camel's head out the flap of the tent.

20

Exit Laughing (Wryly)

Most foreign residents of Rome, with the albatross of a real estate contract around their necks, spend the first six months of their tenancy of a house or apartment trying to forget the agony involved in getting the thing signed, and the last six months worrying about getting safely out of it.

There is the matter of the deposit. This is usually the equivalent of two months' rent, though it may be more or less depending upon the lessee's previous experience with Italian contracts, and the wiliness of the landlord. This deposit is theoretically held in escrow in the hands of a third party pending the safe return of the house and its contents to the owners at the termination of the lease. Deductible from the deposit are any damages which the fiendishly sharp eye of the landlord or his lawyer or agent, or all three, can discern, or the cost of any items missing in the inventory.

Newcomers to the Eternal City innocently assume that the deposit will be returned intact, particularly if they have no unfortunate accessories such as a pet boxer addicted to table legs, or a great aunt with a tendency to kleptomania. At worst, they reason, they can be charged with nothing more than the broken handle of the lavatory (which probably fell apart in their hands the first day they were in the house), and the chip in one of the soup plates in the dinner service.

It is a careless landlord and an unworthy lawyer indeed, however, who cannot run a broken faucet and a chipped soup plate up into a damage claim of several hundred thousand lire, or a sum roughly approximating the total deposit. To return the entire deposit without a struggle would be a reflection upon the stamina and the good sense of landlord and lawyer as well.

Knowing this—and every foreigner in Rome becomes well informed on the subject as it is one of the favorite topics of conversation—the last six months of tenancy are a long drawn out preoccupation with how to get back the deposit. Many, especially those with large living allowances from governments or oil companies, just write the deposit off as a gone goose from the moment they pay it, thus making their landlords very appreciative of their superior intelligence and with a preference thereafter for embassy or oil company employees as tenants.

Others, whose rent and deposit money comes out of the sweat of their brows, are not so ready to relinquish it unchallenged. There are two schools of thought relative to the best method of getting back the deposit. Old timers say, "Live it up." Newcomers protest that this is a violation of the contract which specifically states that the deposit is not to be considered as rent and may not be applied as rent. Old timers say, yes, but the landlord is already in violation (in all probability) of the law in one or both of the following ways: 1, he has not registered the contract for its full value with the government; 2, he has not put the deposit money in escrow in the hands of a third person, but rather has invested it sensibly in some high-interest-bearing project, and hence does not actually have the money in hand to repay the tenant, assuming he can find no damages to charge him with.

Newcomers, if they decide to live up the deposit, usually write the landlord a courteous letter to that effect, whereupon they are given an ultimatum either to continue paying rent to the last or face a law suit. The milquetoasts continue paying—and spend the next several months or years suing the landlord to recover the deposit. In either case it makes work for Rome's many lawyers.

Old timers just quietly go ahead and live it up and ignore the landlord's threats of suit by calling his attention to the above mentioned points in which he himself is caught in a *contravvenzione*.

There are, of course, exceptions, and an occasional owner actually repays the deposit without a fuss and without exorbitant claims for damage. In our own nearly ten years in Rome, during which we have lived in five different parts of the city, we have encountered only one landlord who made no issue over the deposit money. Almost without exception our friends who have come and gone during these years have had to hire lawyers to handle their lease problems.

But when we lived in the House of the Four Winds, we were still ignorant of the ways of Roman landlords. We made the mistake of paying rent up until the last. Pitted against a Scotch-Calabrian combination, however, our landlord was up against a tough proposition. We were determined to get back that deposit money or die in the attempt. Particularly since the vagaries of post-war economy had caused the original 200,000 lire deposit to dwindle to something like $500 from its original $2,000.

When the time came to make the inventory, the landlord went over the house inch by inch and reluctantly came to the conclusion that he could not—as a gentleman—find more than 50,000 lire worth of damages, one lamp having been cracked and repaired, and one ebony wall bracket having fallen and been damaged. He would repay the deposit, he said, just as soon as we paid the 50,000 lire damage bill. At this point Frank cannily confronted him with itemized bills showing repairs made on the house by us which totaled 52,000 lire.

"Shall we not just cancel these two accounts," he asked politely, "and then you can pay me back the deposit at once?"

"It is quite irregular," said the landlord.

"It is reasonable and just," replied Frank.

"I will have to consult my lawyer," said the landlord.

"*Arrivederla.*"

On the morrow the negotiations were again politely resumed.

"It is most irregular," said the landlord.

"It is reasonable and just," replied the tenant evenly.

"I will have to consult my other lawyer," said the landlord.

"*Arrivederla* tomorrow."

Meanwhile we were packed and ready to go, and the negotiations for the return of the 200,000 lire deposit went on.

Came the moment set for our departure. The landlord arrived empty handed but full of explanations as to why he could not see fit to return the 200,000 lire deposit under the circumstances. Very well, we could postpone our departure until he thought the matter over further.

"*Arrivederla* again."

After his departure we loaded our trunks into the truck and sent them into town to the new apartment. The children and I followed. "I," said Frank, "will remain here until he pays me 200,000 lire if it takes all summer."

"*Arrivederci* next fall, then," I said, kissing him goodbye.

For the better part of a week Frank went on quietly occupying the villa, having hired a jobless Italian friend to stay on the premises while he worked. We communicated by telephone and he briefed me on the progress of negotiations. Finally into his office in Rome came the landlord's pretty *Signora* in tears, but with her handbag bulging with 200,000 lire. She made a last dramatic effort to shake the obdurate Brutto.

"You are a hard man, *Signor* Brutto," she said finally. "*Molto, molto duro!*" And she handed over the deposit money, whereupon Frank laid the keys of the villa in her soft little palm and the incident was closed.

"The pleasure," he said to her sweetly, "has been all mine, *Signora.*"

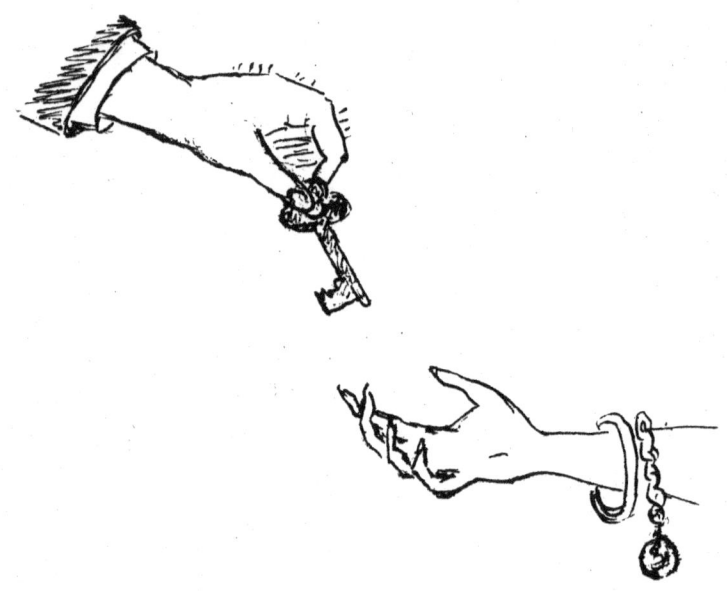

21

Buon Riposo—At Last!

When the time came to move away from the House of the Four Winds, we were eager to go. It was beautiful as it had been in the beginning—more beautiful to us, in fact, for things were arranged to our taste, the furniture glowed with polishing, the floors gleamed with wax. Diffused and silvery the spring sunlight fell through the windows, baywood fires still perfumed the rooms. Yet we were ready to leave without regret.

As I suppose a man discovers at leisure after marriage, mere physical attributes of beauty are rarely enough. If the stunning creature he walked up the aisle with turns out to be a nagging harpy who makes constant unreasonable demands upon his time, his patience, and his pocketbook, he is likely eventually to see her beauty through jaundiced eyes and wonder if, after all, life might not have been pleasanter with that little Jones girl with the buck teeth.

Espoused to this house, which we had taken unto ourselves in such pride and anticipation, our disillusionment increased as we knew it more intimately. We were ready to look for a little apartment with cheap lithographs instead of school-of-Botticelli Madonnas, with fiber rugs instead of Persian, with simple crockery instead of alabaster cups that had been in the family of Napoleon Bonaparte. We would be grateful, too, if the roof, though neither lofty nor extensive, held out the winter rain.

I remembered other leave-takings and I reflected that in almost every instance circumstances had conspired to make departure less a sorrow than a relief. Situations tend to serve their purpose in our lives and then disintegrate. Change is implicit. Things are not what they were. A tree is felled outside the window and exposes a city dump. A factory is built across the way. An undesirable tenant clatters overhead. A pet dies, a relative departs. Joy is diminished in a thousand subtle ways. Better to move along. Everything we love best goes with us, anyway. The striking of a hall clock chimes on in the memory, the mellow gleam of old wood is a luster in the heart.

And so parting from the villa was made easy, and I suppose even thus, at the end of his lease on mortality, a man can be reconciled to his ultimate departure. The old habitation gets a bit leaky in the roof, shaky in the foundations. Its plumbing can be kept functioning only by constant attention from the experts at great expense. It was a fine, airy place on the good days, he reflects, full of warmth and laughter—but the house-guests are gone now, and oh, the icy drafts in winter! It had birdsong and fire-light and the ticking of a clock—but dust from the inexorable termites keeps sifting down from the rafters.

Cosi sia. The weary and disillusioned tenant is ready to surrender the keys of the big house, ready to settle for a room with a view—a narrow room that opens on the wide, calm vista of eternity.

As for us, departing from the House of the Four Winds, we were glad to settle for a six-room apartment in town. How simple everything was. A bath adjacent to each bedroom. Central heating. A *portiere* to worry about intruders. Common old furniture whose total value was less than that of one room at the villa. No old masters. No priceless antiques. We even looked with affection at the hideous portrait of the *padrona* that dominated one wall of the living room.

When Frank eventually joined us there after his week of holding out for the return of the deposit on the villa, he climbed into his pajamas with a look of intense relief.

"Well," he said, "*buon riposo.*"

"Just repeat that slowly," I said. "Just say it again. It has such a lovely, restful sound…"

"*Buon riposo!*"

ABOUT THE AUTHOR

Sallie Sinclair Maclay grew up on a Montana ranch, and met her future husband, Frank Brutto, in the University's School of Journalism. When their first child was just three months old, Frank was assigned to Europe as a War Correspondent. After five long years of separation, the young family was reunited at last in post-war Italy, where they made their home for the next sixteen years. Sallie passed away in 1992, leaving behind the unpublished manuscript of *The Lady Is Delicate*.